REDEFINING ◄

General Education

► IN THE

► AMERICAN

► HIGH

► SCHOOL

Arthur D. Roberts and Gordon Cawelti

About the Authors

Arthur D. Roberts is Professor of Education, Curriculum and Instruction, University of Connecticut, Storrs.

Gordon Cawelti is Executive Director, Association for Supervision and Curriculum Development, Alexandria, Virginia.

Editing: Ronald S. Brandt, *ASCD Executive Editor*
Jo Ann Irick, Nancy Carter Modrak, and Anne Roney, *Staff Editors*

Cover design: Al Way, *ASCD Art Director*

Photography: Christine L. Roberts

**Price:** $8.50
ASCD Stock Number: 611-84332
ISBN: 0-87120-126-7
Library of Congress Card Catalog Number: 84-71655

Contents

Foreword

America's schools have been the focus of numerous reports in the last two years. Panels, commissions, and researchers have proposed long lists of reforms, including frequent recommendations for increasing the number of courses required for high school graduation. Noticeably absent from most of these reports has been extended consideration of the content of these added requirements. Also missing from most of them was any suggestion that the professional educators who spend their days in direct contact with students might know something about what those students could and should learn.

The ASCD project reported in this book was different. It was launched several years ago to address a problem later identified in other reports: the curriculum of most high schools is an uncoordinated jumble of departments and courses. Each piece has its own rationale for inclusion in a total set of offerings, but few school faculties can show how the pieces are related or can explain clearly to students, parents, and others what all students are expected to learn and why.

Some might contend that since educators allowed this confusion to develop, they cannot be trusted to straighten it out. On the contrary, ASCD believed that with encouragement and stimulation from a respected association, and membership in a national network, teams of local educators could play a leading role in redesigning their own general education programs.

This book reports on a series of visits made by Arthur Roberts to each of the participating schools. It is not really a final report, because the process is continuing — as it should. However, the results so far amply demonstrate the soundness of ASCD's emphasis on cooperative curriculum development and our faith in the good judgment of principals and teachers.

PHIL C. ROBINSON
President, 1984-85
Association for Supervision
and Curriculum Development

Acknowledgments

Thanks to the teachers, administrators, students, and parents in the ASCD network who supplied me with reports, opinions, and gracious answers to endless questions.

Thanks to Christine L. Roberts, my colleague, traveling companion, photographer, and editor-of-first-resort.

ARTHUR D. ROBERTS

1 Origins of the Network

The early 1980s heralded a revival of interest in the American high school, particularly with regard to basic skills deficiencies. This interest was not new. In the late 50s, many schools responded to the recommendations of the Conant report, which advocated comprehensive high schools. In my own analysis of major reports by commissions or groups in the early 70s, I concluded that their primary focus was on developing alternative routes to graduation and on problems associated with the transition from schooling to the world of work.[1] Only limited attention was given to the curriculum in general or graduation requirements in particular.

Today, concerns about ill-prepared high school graduates are being expressed by employers as well as university faculty members, who are increasingly required to provide remedial instruction in composition and reading skills. There is also uncertainty about major changes in life styles and in the work world, where people are likely to see significant alterations in employment patterns. Some forecasters, such as Marvin Cetron,[2] anticipate a "high-tech" future resulting in several hundred thousand jobs in such areas as robotry repair, laser technology, computer programming, and geriatrics. This forecast, however, contrasts sharply with Bureau of Labor Statistics data showing that most future jobs will be nontechnical—salesclerks, cashiers, secretaries, waiters, and janitors. Indeed, the Bureau predicts that by 1990 new technical jobs will account for only 8 percent of the total new job growth.[3]

The employment scenario has been further complicated by an oversupply of college graduates. One recent longitudinal study[4] reported that of 20,000 1972 high school graduates who later received a college degree, 43 percent in 1979 were doing work that did not require a four-year degree.

Behind the various analyses of statistics on education and employment is the assumption that a fundamental purpose of the high school is to prepare students for the work world. Indeed, reports appearing in 1983 and 1984 laid blame at the doors of the school for the decline of productivity in America.

> Our once unchallenged preeminence in commerce, industry, science, and technological innovation is being overtaken by competition throughout the world.[5]

This statement from the Commission on Excellence was echoed in other reports, although rarely, if ever, had schools earlier been given credit for U.S. superiority. (Since when has it been the job of schools to provide training in strategic planning—which might have told General Motors to start making smaller cars sooner than they did—or in quality control or technological innovation?)

At the turn of the decade the political response had emerged in various organizational or control mechanisms such as accountability plans, minimum competency testing of students, and interest in so-called "life skills" needed by all students. While the urgency of improving basic skill attainment could not be underestimated, it was becoming apparent that these legislative actions could very easily result in a trivialized secondary education. Such an education would fall far short of the much nobler purposes long espoused for precollegiate education. The time had come for a significant national effort to provide leadership in defining what a forward-looking program of general education should be for the American high school.

Selecting Network Schools

I first discussed the necessity for such leadership at the 1980 convention of the National Association of Secondary School Principals.[6] I found that high school principals and other school leaders shared my concern about general education. I felt then, as I do now, that "optionalizing" the secondary school had produced a patchwork curriculum at the expense of a well-designed program of general education for all students. General education typically consumes from half to three-fourths of the high school years, as opposed to specialized education, which may be vocational or college preparatory.

In October 1980, ASCD's Executive Council authorized funds for a project to redefine general education in the American high school.[7] The Association subsequently received additional funds from the Ford Foundation for program support and from the Johnson Foundation for hosting meetings at the Wingspread Conference Center in Racine, Wisconsin.

ASCD then issued a call for interested high schools to participate in the project for two years, during which they would be part of a network of schools designated to receive help in reconceptualizing their existing general education programs. This school-based network was founded on the belief that local faculties engaged in curriculum development would come to feel a strong sense of ownership in the results. Further, such work would be more enduring than legislative mandates or a public response to a plethora of national reports. To ensure the involvement of major stakeholders and to reflect ASCD's commitment to cooperative curriculum planning, applicant schools were expected to send teams including school board members, the superintendent or an assistant superintendent, the principal, and a teacher representative.

In May 1981, a committee chaired by Daniel Tanner of Rutgers University met with me, as Project Director, and Jim Keefe of NASSP to select the participating schools. We took extreme care to select high schools representative of various regions of the country, those with a high rate of college-bound students, as well as schools with a low-college-bound rate so that the network would include typical kinds of high schools. Our final selection included 17 schools, 14 of which are described in Chapter 2.

Activities of the Network

The primary purpose of the network was to facilitate local faculty and community study of existing general education programs in order to design a comprehensive and balanced curriculum appropriate to the lives of students in the years ahead. A secondary but closely related purpose was to provide various perspectives on the future in order to determine what knowledge is of most worth.

To these ends, network meetings focused on the issues of curriculum balance and content or process issues in specific fields. Participants interacted with presenters, reported on approaches they were taking in their own schools, and shared problems they were encountering.

The kickoff meeting of the network was held at Wingspread in July 1981, with former Commissioner of Education Ernest Boyer discussing his views on the nature of common learnings, which he and his colleagues at the Carnegie Foundation had articulated. Harry Broudy and I presented other conceptualizations on broad fields of knowledge. Also discussed at that first network meeting were various change strategies. Terrence Deal of Harvard urged that teams carefully and thoroughly elicit all faculty members' views once the study got under way.

At subsequent meetings the group heard other well-known speakers and writers who presented a range of viewpoints, all of whom aided network members as they deliberated on a model for general education they could use in their respective schools. Mortimer Adler, for instance, discussed his Paideia proposal for a common classics curriculum for all youth. Robert Bundy emphasized futures planning and suggested that schools help students develop a new set of values for contending with life in the next century. Herman Kahn discussed a Hudson Institute program that helps teachers engage students in the analysis of complex global issues such as nuclear warfare, hunger and poverty, and changing economic cycles. This kind of analysis, Kahn believed, helps youth develop less pessimistic attitudes about the future.

Presentations were also made by Ted Sizer, who reported on his study of high schools, and R. Freeman Butts, who discussed the central role of civic education in American schools. Attention to the development of common learnings within specific subject fields was provided by Jeremiah Reedy, Professor of Classics at Macalester College, who described his work with Minnesota high schools in developing unified humanities programs. James Robinson of the University of Colorado made suggestions for integrating concepts of technology into general education science programs. And Scott Thomson, Director of the National Association of Secondary School Principals, addressed the changing expectations of the high school over the decades.

These presentations stimulated much discussion and directed the teams' attention to central purposes and what they meant for general education in their schools. But just as important was the support provided by group interaction during network meetings: members saw that their own restraints and difficulties were similar to those of other faculties and communities. Valuable as the network meetings were, they were relatively brief compared with the hundreds of hours participants spent back in their home districts discussing what their newly acquired information meant in terms of curriculum revision.

Concepts of General Education

Through the decades several significant formulations of general education have been suggested for high schools. For the most part, these models represented various individual or committee views on how to cluster knowledge into broad fields. They appeared more alike than different. Typically, they suggested that knowledge is interdisciplinary; yet there is little evidence of this in schools, where the curriculum continues to be divided into traditional subject-matter courses limited to a single field, such as history or science.

During the 1930s, the famous Eight-Year Study inspired several high schools to develop a more integrated core curriculum that focused on both societal issues and the needs of youth. Despite the success of these experiments, any broader dissemination eventually gave way to traditional subject-matter courses.

The following is a brief chronology of significant recommendations on general education that have appeared in recent decades.

1945 *The Harvard Committee*[8] recommended that at least half of school time be spent on a core curriculum consisting of three units of mathematics and science, three units of English, and two units of social studies. The committee's report acknowledged the different needs of college-bound students and those entering vocations; they likened general education to the five fingers of the hand branching out somewhat differently for various students.

1959 *The Conant Report*[9] is generally regarded as having reaffirmed the usefulness of the comprehensive high school, which had been under some attack. The report recommended four years of study in English, three or four in social studies, and one each in mathematics and science. Conant also recommended that the core curriculum consume half or more of the student's time.

1964 *Broudy, Smith, and Burnett clusters*[10] reflected more concern for broad fields than specific subject courses and recommended that high schools develop instructional experiences for all youth within five areas:
1. Symbolics of information such as English, foreign language, and mathematics.
2. Basic sciences in traditional subject areas.
3. Developmental studies including the evolution of cultures and social institutions.
4. Exemplars in art, music, drama, and literature with emphasis more on appreciation of the arts than performance.
5. Molar social problems (similar to Conant's recommendation for a contemporary problems course for seniors).

1980 Former U.S. Commissioner of Education Ernest Boyer and his colleague, Art Levine, said in their *Common Learnings*[11] proposal that while we are a diverse and pluralistic nation, we share many common concerns, including (1) relationship with nature, (2) values and beliefs, (3) membership in groups and institutions, (4) use of symbols, (5) sense of time, and (6) producing and consuming. Boyer and Levine proposed that these concepts be developed into appropriate instructional experiences within required subject areas.

1982 *Cawelti's General Education Model*[12] retained a broad fields subject identification, but principally recognized that high schools now accept a fundamental responsibility for ensuring a clear sequence of instructional experiences in "learning, thinking, and communicating skills." While high schools in earlier decades did not usually teach reading, evidence was persuasive that they needed to continue instruction in reading as well as other fundamental learning skills. The model proposed integrating key concepts into citizenship-societal studies, cultural studies, and science-technology clusters (see Figure 1).

1983 *College Board Competencies and Content*.[13] An outgrowth of the College Entrance Examination Board's long-term Educational EQuality Project, *Academic Preparation for College* presented the collaborative efforts of university scholars and secondary school teachers to define competencies needed for success in college. These competencies included reading, writing, speaking and listening, mathematics, reasoning, and studying. The booklet also listed general content preferences in English, the arts, mathematics, science, social studies, and foreign language.

1983 *Carnegie Study*.[14] Ernest Boyer's *High School* recommended that approximately two thirds of the high school curriculum be common to all students. The proposal favored a more balanced approach than other reports because it included foreign language, a semester course on technology, and one in the arts, plus a work seminar and an independent project for seniors (see Figure 2). The report also recommended that all schools require community service of their students.

1984 *Goodlad's Time Allocations*.[15] Goodlad recommended that the following percentages of time be allocated to various fields, somewhat along the lines of the Harvard report: literature and language, 18 percent; mathematics and science, 18 percent; social studies, 15 percent; arts, 15 percent; vocations, 15 percent; and physical education, 10 percent. Goodlad also called for spending more time on a core curriculum reflecting balance among the major areas.

Both in their local schools and at network meetings, program participants gave careful consideration to time allocations for each subject area. Most of the national reports listed above came out after the schools had conducted extensive deliberations and most had decided on a general education model. Thus, the network schools were ahead of the game by the time *A Nation at Risk* appeared in the spring of 1983, and network representatives were already informing other schools about the process the network had used to redefine core curriculum.

A Nation at Risk proposed a "new basics" curriculum that consisted

Figure 1. The Gordon Cawelti Model for High School General Education

Cultural Studies

Subjects:

Literature
Language Arts
Art
Music
Drama
Humanities
Philosophy
Religion
Film Criticism
Architecture
Ethnic Studies
Foreign Language

Concepts, Issues, Topics:

Historical Relevance
Performance
Critical Consumption
Creative Expression

Citizenship—Societal Studies

Subjects:

History   Economics
Government   Sociology
Law-Related Education   Psychology
                         Geography

Concepts, Issues, Topics:

Evaluate Issues   Civil Rights
Participation Skills   Ecology
Rights and Responsibilities Population
Global Interdependence   Disarmament
Institutions
Poverty

Learning—Communicating—Thinking Skills

Mathematics
Composition
Speaking
Listening
Reading
Reasoning
Problem Solving
Critical Thinking
Computer Literacy
Locational Skills

Science—Technology

Subjects:

Biology
Physics
Chemistry
Physiology
Earth Science
Genetics
Anthropology

Concepts, Issues, Topics:

Nuclear Energy
Technology and Work
Conservation
Resource Scarcity
Genetic Engineering

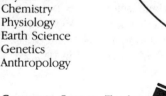

Health—Recreation—Leisure

Subjects:

Physical Education
Health
Science
Home Economics

Concepts, Issues, Topics:

Fitness
Sex Education
Drug Education
Parenting
Coping
Lifetime Sports

of three years of both science and mathematics, four years of English, three years of social studies, and a course on computer use. Most of the network schools settled on a two-year requirement in science and mathematics. The network's Florida school was compelled by state legislation to adopt the three-year requirement. Similarly, network schools in other states were also required by legislative action to adopt changes they probably would not have made if left to their own counsel.

Figure 2. Ernest Boyer's Proposed Core of Common Learnings

		Academic Units
Language:	5 units	
	Basic English: Writing	1
	Speech	1/2
	Literature	1
	Foreign Language	2
	Arts	1/2
History:	2-1/2 units	
	U.S. History	1
	Western Civilization	1
	Non-Western Studies	1/2
Civics:	1 unit	1
Science:	2 units	
	Physical Science	1
	Biological Science	1
Mathematics		2
Technology		1/2
Health		1/2
Seminar on Work		1/2
Senior Independent Project		1/2
	Total	14-1/2

Settling on the number of years to be required for each subject area proved to be less time consuming than defining the common learnings that were to be incorporated into the various required courses. The network schools typically came up with 100 or more of these common learnings as they further defined the five or six broad fields or clusters of their general education model. And once the common learnings were fully developed, local faculties were faced with ensuring that they were actually taught to all students at some point in the core curriculum.

Approaches to Determining What Knowledge Is of Most Worth

Most of the major reports appearing in 1983 and 1984 carried recommendations on the core curriculum that simply reflected some individual or group's opinion on what subjects or content should be taught to all students. In general, they called for *more* academic courses, whether students were bound for college or the work world. This was not the case in the Sizer[16] study, which argued that "less is more" and that students should be given maximum help in attaining competency in basic literacy and mathematical skills before proceeding into concentrated study in four broad areas: (1) inquiry and expression, (2) mathematics and science, (3) literature and the arts, and (4) philosophy and history.

Aside from particular values expressed by various individuals on what this core should be, other classical and empirical approaches may be taken in selecting content to be taught. The *scholarly judgment* of experts in various fields has been a prominent resource. Two decades ago, for instance, the National Science Foundation called upon scholars in its efforts to reform science and mathematics textbooks. Panels of university and school personnel carefully analyzed their fields to ascertain which concepts held the greatest potential and applicability for inclusion in textbooks.

Studying adult needs was an important approach taken many years ago to determine which reading words, spelling words, or mathematical competencies were likely to be most useful in later life. Outside these basic areas, however, little research has been done that would be of value to the curriculum developer. How does one decide what science, or history, or literature can be expected to be of most utility to adults? The ASCD network interjected this kind of thinking through the future perspectives provided by Kahn and Bundy at network meetings; but, with the possible exception of an emphasis on "higher order thinking skills," it had had minimal effect. If one seriously examines increasing world tension and the alternative life styles already followed by middle class youth unable to connect with conventional economic levels of attainment, then surely the advice of Kahn and Bundy deserves serious consideration.

These concerns lead to examination of the *societal needs* approach in selecting common content and learning experiences. A majority of the resolutions passed each year at the ASCD Annual Conference fall within the "social issues" arena, including such areas as pluralism, sexism, and peaceful uses of nuclear power as legitimate concerns of schooling. A very different mission for schools would appear if societal needs were the organizing elements of the curriculum.

In a much less philosophical vein, the impact of *textbooks and testing instruments* is probably the most powerful influence on the curriculum. The authors of textbooks are, of course, influenced by societal or adult needs and by the work of scholars, but the multiplicity of demands on publishers has led to increasingly bland materials that would greatly disappoint the social reconstructionists and others interested in teaching controversial subjects in the schools.

As for testing, instructional programs in New York have for many years been greatly influenced by the Regents' examination, and the impact of terminal examinations is bound to increase even more as states adopt a variety of competency tests. Surely the testing tail is wagging the dog in many communities.

In summary, network meetings occupied relatively little time over the two years of the project, but many significant persons with powerful ideas stimulated network members' thinking. Even more important were the lengthy deliberations in the local communities as schools redefined their general education programs. The fascinating events that took place during those months are chronicled by Art Roberts in the following chapters.

2 The Schools

The ASCD networks schools represent a wide cross section of American communities: the affluent, the middle class, the poor, and some that include a range of socioeconomic backgrounds (see Figure 3). The schools are located in inner cities (East High School in Denver and O. Perry Walker High School in New Orleans); in large county systems (Baltimore County's Woodlawn High School and Pinellas County's Pinellas Park High School); in suburbs (Oak Park and River Forest High School, San Rafael High School, and Scarsdale High School); in college towns (Ames High School and Huron and Pioneer High Schools in Ann Arbor); and in small towns and cities (Carlsbad High School, Page High School, and Buena and Ventura High Schools). The populations of these schools also reflect our nation's ethnic diversity. While most of the schools show an Anglo majority, two are predominantly black, one is predominantly Navaho, and one has a 60 percent-40 percent Anglo-Hispanic mix.

The schools vary considerably in size, from Page's 725 students to Oak Park and River Forest's 3,360 (see Figure 4 for a summary of data on the 14 schools that had completed the network project by early 1984[1]). The majority of the schools include grades 9-12, but for some this is a recent pattern that resulted from declining enrollments and the need to consolidate programs and/or schools.

Most of the network schools are comprehensive high schools, with Scarsdale's college preparatory program the most notable of a few exceptions. These schools send more of their graduates on to further education than does the average American high school, which sends approximately 50-60 percent of its graduates on to college. This statistic is not difficult to understand. As New Orleans Assistant Super-

Figure 3. Network Participants

1. Ames Senior High school
   Ames, Iowa

2. Ann Arbor Huron High School
   Ann Arbor, Michigan

3. Ann Arbor Pioneer High School
   Ann Arbor, Michigan

4. Buena High School
   Ventura, California

5. Carlsbad High School
   Carlsbad, New Mexico

6. Central High School
   St. Louis, Missouri

7. Colville High School
   Colville, Washington

8. East High School
   Denver, Colorado

9. O. Perry Walker High School
   New Orleans, Louisiana

10. Oak Park and River Forest High School
    Oak Park, Illinois

11. Page High School
    Page, Arizona

12. Pinellas Park High School
    Largo, Florida

13. San Rafael High School
    San Rafael, California

14. Scarsdale High School
    Scarsdale, New York

15. Ventura High School
    Ventura, California

16. Will Rogers High School
    Tulsa, Oklahoma

17. Woodlawn Senior High School
    Baltimore, Maryland

intendent Julianna Boudreaux remarked in her interview with us,

> This group of schools in some ways is a very above average group of
> schools. First, they applied for membership in the network, which
> suggests a strong sense of self-worth; and second, when a large system
> such as New Orleans applies for inclusion in a national program such as
> ASCD's, they usually pick an outstanding school, as New Orleans did
> when it chose O. Perry Walker High School.

We understood what she meant after learning that we had been
preceded in several of these high schools by visiting Japanese educators who had come to see what is going on in America's better high
schools. Having read in many publications that Japanese high schools
are superior to ours, teachers in these network schools wondered why
Japanese educators were visiting them. Is it possible that in a few years
our social critics will call for a new parity with Japanese education?
And will the parity depend on techniques that the Japanese saw here
on their visits?

Figure 4 also includes information about the faculties of the 14
schools, including the percentage of teachers holding a Master's degree or higher and the number of teachers holding doctorates. Predictably, Oak Park and River Forest and Scarsdale, which have the
largest number of teachers holding doctorates, also show the highest
maximum salaries (over $40,000).

If there were such a thing as an "average" school in the network, it
would have 1,784 students, a faculty of 107 teachers, 72 percent of
whom hold an M.A. degree or higher, with four holding doctorates.
The ethnic mix in the school would be approximately 71 percent
Anglo, 15 percent black, 6 percent Hispanic, 4 percent Native American, 2 percent Asian, and 2 percent other. Eight students per school
would be National Merit finalists, and 67 percent of the graduating
class in each school would pursue further study in either a two- or
four-year college or university.

Statistics are interesting; but they don't tell much about the unique-
ness of this group of high schools, each of which has its own distinct
identity. To get a better sense of the schools, the remainder of this
chapter includes a brief description of each community and descrip-
tive comments about the network high schools in these communities.

Figure 4. Profile of the Network Schools

	School Size	Grades	Ethnic Composition	Post-Graduation Education	National Merit Finalists	Annual Per Pupil Expenditure	Faculty Members	Percentage Faculty With M.A. or Higher	Faculty With Ph.D.
Ames	1,120	10-12	Anglo: 93% Asian: 3% Black: 1% Other: 3%	4 year: 61% 2 year: 15%	14	2,600	77	77%	4
Ann Arbor: Huron	1,742	10-12	Anglo: 78% Asian: 3% Black: 18% Other: 1%	81%	13	3,742	123	85%	3
Ann Arbor: Pioneer	1,658	10-12	Anglo: 79% Asian: 3% Black: 16% Other: 2%	75%	14	3,742	105	79%	5
Woodlawn	1,838	9-12	Anglo: 49% Black: 50% Other: 1%	4 year: 21% 2 year: 26% Tech./Voc.: 17%	4	3,300	119	78%	3
Carlsbad	1,483	10-12	Anglo: 58% Black: 2.3% Hispanic: 39.7%	College/Univ.: 40.7% Tech./Voc.: 2.7%	2	2,216	82	60%	0
East	1,930	9-12	Anglo: 50% Asian: 4% Black: 36% Hispanic: 9% Native Amer.: 1%	4 year: 62% 2 year: 9% Tech./Voc.: 8%	3 Finalists 2 Recipients	3,709	98	85%	4

District	Enrollment	Grades	Ethnic breakdown	Post-graduation					
Oak Park and River Forest	3,360	9-12	Anglo: 80% Black: 15% Other: 5%	4 year: 60% 2 year/other: 20%	15	4,365	257	90%	13
Page	725	9-12	Anglo: 46% Native Amer.: 52% Other: 2%	20%	1983-1 1984-0	3,000	39	50%	0
Pinellas Park	2,200	9-12	Anglo: 88.5% Black: 10% Other: 1.5%	4 year: 38% 2 year: 20% Voc./Tech.: 14%	2	2,287	115	44%	2
San Rafael	1,150	9-12	Anglo: 86% Asian: 5% Black: 3% Hispanic: 5% Native Amer.: 1%	4 year: 39% 2 year/other: 53%	1983-4 1984-0	2,550	55	55%	2
Ventura: Buena	2,400	9-12	Anglo: 77% Asian: 2.6% Black: 1% Hispanic: 15.3% Other: 4.1%	4 year: 26% 2 year: 39%	2	2,345	100	75%	0
Ventura	1,992	9-12	Anglo: 86% Black: 1.5% Hispanic: 11% Other: 1.5%	4 year: 30% 2 year: 30%	2	2,345	115	78%	0
O. Perry Walker	1,775	9-12	Anglo: 35% Black: 59% Hispanic: 1% Other: 5%	65-70%	3	2,164	90	50%	2
Scarsdale	1,600	9-12	Anglo: 90% Asian: 7-8% Other: 2%	4 year: 91% 2 year: 4% Voc./Tech.: 2%	37	5,800	122	96%	14

Ames, Iowa

Ames is located 35 miles north of Des Moines, the Iowa state capital, and has a population of 45,775. A large proportion of the parents in the community are college graduates employed in business and the professions. Over 3,000 people are employed in the professions and over 7,500 in government. Ames is the home of the Iowa State University, the Iowa State Department of Transportation, the National Disease Laboratory, and numerous other governmental and private agencies.

Ames High School—the town's only high school—is a three-year comprehensive high school that emphasizes college preparation. Last year, of the 152 junior, middle, and high schools recognized in the United States under the Department of Education's Secondary School Recognition Program, only Ames had all of its secondary schools honored. Students in the high school characterize Ames as a university town and their high school as "loaded with good teachers who have very high expectations for us." Teachers teach five periods a day and, in most cases, are available during a sixth designated period to give help to any students who need it.

As was true in several of the project schools, the Ames project enjoyed strong support from its superintendent and individual school board members. A close working relationship between the Ames High School Principal Ralph Farrar and Assistant Superintendent Lu Kiser enabled the entire system to benefit from the ASCD project.

Ann Arbor, Michigan

Ann Arbor is located 45 miles west of Detroit and has a population of 106,000. It is the home of one of the nation's premier institutions of higher learning, the University of Michigan, which was founded in 1837. Ann Arbor is also a university town as well as the home of light industry and a number of government and private research laboratories, which have earned Ann Arbor the title, "Research Center of the Midwest." The high school's faculty told us that Ann Arbor is one of Michigan's most expensive communities in which to live. People are willing to shoulder heavy real estate payments because the town and university have so much to offer. Executives who work in Detroit see Ann Arbor as an exclusive address and are willing to commute the 45 miles to the city so that their families can enjoy the benefits of the community.

Both teachers and administrators described the community as being pro-education, even though the system receives practically no state aid because of its tax base.

Ann Arbor opened the first publicly supported secondary school in Michigan in 1856 (at a cost of $32,000). Today it has three high schools, two of which—Huron and Pioneer—were part of the ASCD network. Huron, the younger of the two high schools, was established in 1969, only a few years before Ann Arbor's high school enrollments peaked with approximately 5,300 students.

Huron High School serves a section of Ann Arbor that includes both low-income housing and some of the community's most expensive homes. Although Ann Arbor's high school population has decreased from its peak, Huron's enrollment is holding steady. Its distinguished staff, many of whom came to Huron when it opened, includes the two 1983 Presidential Award winners (math and science) selected in Michigan.

Each grade (10-12) in Huron and Pioneer has its own full-time administrator, two counselors, and a secretary. Each principal stays with a class until it graduates. As part of their responsibilities, these principals handle discipline problems, although there is also a schoolwide assistant principal in charge of general discipline, scheduling, and the Advanced Placement Program. Huron personnel were especially proud of their Advanced Placement Program, which involved 167 students last year, 93 percent of whom earned college credit for their efforts. Huron has a program of peer counseling, and students are given training to help them to participate in this program.

The school is also proud of its vocational program, especially its nationally recognized work in graphic arts. Most students who do well are able to get jobs in the field upon completion of the program. Graduates of this program have also gone on to the best graphic arts college programs in the country.

Pioneer High School, located in a well-established part of Ann Arbor, is the older and the smaller of the two schools. Unlike Huron, it has seen decline in enrollment. In many cases, the parents of today's students themselves attended Pioneer. For many years it was the preparatory school for the University of Michigan. It was the first high school in Michigan to have a planetarium, one of the first in the Midwest to have an Advanced Placement Program, and also one of the first to have an interdisciplinary program in the humanities. Among Pioneer's many successful graduates is astronaut Jack Lousman, a member of the class of 1964.

As might be expected, there is a healthy rivalry between the two schools. We sensed this competition in our conversations with teachers and administrators at the two schools. We hasten to add that we also saw a high level of mutual respect as the faculties of the two schools continue to cooperate on the ASCD project.

Baltimore County, Maryland

Woodlawn Senior High School, one of 21 high schools in Baltimore County, Maryland, is the district's representative to the ASCD network. Baltimore County is one of the 25 largest school systems in the country with approximately 84,000 students (down from 132,000 in 1973), 30,000 of whom are high school students. Covering 610 square miles of diverse geography, neighborhoods, and life styles, Baltimore County, shaped much like a horeshoe, surrounds the city of Baltimore on three sides. The county contains no incorporated towns or cities. It has one single school system, which is divided into five administrative areas, each with an assistant superintendent.

Since the entire county had already begun an examination of its high school program when it applied for membership in the ASCD network, it selected a typical high school as its proposed representative. Woodlawn Senior High School is a microcosm of life in the county, a school with students from farms and suburbs and some students who formerly attended school in the city of Baltimore. It is best described as a comprehensive high school.

The school, we were told by a guidance counselor, has an "affluent mentality," but in reality it is not affluent at all. Like other county schools, Woodlawn is linked with area colleges, and the business department works with an advisory committee from the community to help build programs for the world of work. This advisory committee helps answer questions such as, "What does a computer operator need to know in the business world?" The school's "key citizen program" improves communication with the community by inviting citizens who do not have children in school to visit the school to keep informed.

The school has a strong tradition in curriculum development and in guidance (which is considered part of the curriculum, as it is in Pinellas Park). Students are told that the school has a lot to offer so "use your time here as best you can."

Students who are interested in vocational education can attend the Western Vocational Technical Center (one of three vocational/technical centers in the county) for work in any of the 24 vocational areas for half of the school day. Upon graduation from the program, students can present to potential employers a collection of competency profiles in the areas they have mastered.

Carlsbad, New Mexico

Carlsbad Municipal School District is a single high school district that also includes 11 elementary schools, two grade 6-7 middle schools, and one grade 8-9 junior high. The schools serve a multiracial, multicultural community of 33,000 people.

Located on the banks of the Pecos River in southeastern New Mexico and in a corner of the state that was largely unoccupied until the 1870s, Carlsbad is the center of an agricultural area rich in alfalfa and cotton. The school takes its nickname—the Cavemen—from the nearby Carlsbad Caverns. The Caverns are an important factor in the area's economy, as are the potash industry, oil and natural gas production, and the Department of Energy's Waste Isolation Project for storage of nuclear waste material.

School financing comes through the state, with revenues generally financed by a state income tax and taxes on oil and natural gas. With the current abundant supply of oil, schools in New Mexico have faced cuts in their revenues. Consequently, teachers in Carlsbad did not receive salary increases this year.

In spite of hard times, Carlsbad still strives for improvement. The school system has a five-year plan, and the district's school administration has tried to make the townspeople aware of broader horizons for their children. Two goals are to lower the dropout rate and to raise youngsters' expectations about what they might do with their lives.

The *Carlsbad High School* complex was one of the most striking that we saw on our tour. The classrooms and offices in the main building are built on several levels around a central courtyard that is open at one end. Fountains on the first and third levels give the impression of a pleasant oasis or a courtyard in a Moorish castle in southern Spain.

Denver, Colorado

The Mile High City of Denver, which has a city population of approximately 500,000 and over 1,600,000 in the metropolitan area, is one of the nation's major cosmopolitan centers. The discovery of gold—first at Cherry Creek in 1858 and later at Clear Creek in 1859—brought prosperity to the well-positioned hamlets of Auraria and Denver City, which consolidated to become Denver in 1860 and the capital of Colorado Territory in 1861. Soon linked by rail to the rest of the country, Denver grew rapidly and is today one of the country's major manufacturing, transportation, distribution, and tourist centers with a wide range of cultural and recreational advantages, as well as some of the disadvantages common to many major urban areas. As one teacher deftly described it, "We don't have dirty air here; it's just 'used'."

East High traces it origins to 1875. That was the year James H. Balser came from Maine to be principal of the high school section of the Arapahoe School and to teach Greek and physical science. Old East High School was completed in 1889, and the present structure—known for many years as "New" East—opened for classes in 1925. The school's central tower was loosely modeled after Old Hall in Oxford, England, and the overall building resembles Philadelphia's Independence Hall.

For many years East High was Denver's Preparatory School, and elements of that tradition still exist. Upon entering the school and climbing the central staircase, a visitor first sees an impressive replica of Michelangelo's *David,* one of many such replicas brought to Denver many years ago by wealthy Denverites who wanted to expose their children to Europe's best art.

Today, East High, as the school's final report described it, is "an urban school with a large transient population encompassing a broad socioeconomic distribution." What that means, we were told, is that "this school is a real microcosm. We get a full range of kids, from those who are on a free lunch to those who drive to school in their Mercedes. We still get kids, including the governor's son, who leave private schools to come here in the 10th grade."

The school's strong sense of tradition and diverse population, we were informed, are its keys to success. As in so many of the network schools, there was a strong sense of pride here. However, some people think this pride makes change harder to bring about: "We resent change, but it's coming slowly."

Among the unique attributes of the school was a program suggested by teachers five years ago, the Classroom Size Relief Program. Teachers contribute 1/2 of 1 percent of their salary to a special fund used to hire aides, paraprofessionals, and tutors in areas where city funds are not available. The attempt is to get the greatest good for the greatest number, so a building committee using a weighted formula prioritizes the needs and decides how the money will be spent. This was the first time we had heard of such a program.

Department heads at the school are elected by teachers, subject to the principal's approval, and serve a three-year term to which they can be re-elected once. The collective department heads comprise the school's Curriculum Council. They teach a full schedule with one period set aside during which they perform their council duties.

New Orleans, Louisiana

With a city population of approximately 560,000 and a metropolitan area population of 1,200,000, New Orleans is slightly larger than Denver and, at an elevation of 35 feet, almost a mile lower. New Orleans belonged first to France, then to Spain, then to France again under Napoleon. It was eventually sold to the United States as part of the Louisiana Purchase. By 1840, it was the fourth largest city in the country.

However, a rich political history was only part of the city's story. The early French and Spanish settlers created a gracious Creole cultural whose influence is still alive. We sometimes forget that in addition to being a major tourist destination New Orleans is the second largest port in the United States, responsible for 10 percent of foreign trade. It is also a major center of higher education.

New Orleans has 28 high schools, 18 of which are comprehensive. *O. Perry Walker High School,* named after a former New Orleans superintendent of schools, is located on the west bank of the Mississippi River in the part of the city known as Algiers. The high school was established in 1970 and for years was thought of as a "silk-stocking school," an image it no longer claims. The school population has changed, student mobility is higher than it used to be, and fewer students are college-bound now than when the school first opened.

Unlike many schools in the network, O. Perry Walker had a fairly young faculty. Students and teachers alike were proud of the fact that O. Perry Walker is a truly integrated school in a system where most high schools are 90 percent black. Approximately 40 percent of the teachers are black. The excellence of the school's programs and faculty has been the major attraction to students of all the races. In its first ten years, Walker graduated more than 50 Merit Scholars and two Presidential Scholars. In applying for membership in the ASCD project, Principal Bob Gaut's hope was that the network experience could benefit the entire school system.

The school has a Naval ROTC Program (from the school grounds you can see the tops of ships jutting over the Mississippi levee), a business partnership with both a corporation and the power company, and six parent organizations. Its vocational education program includes offerings in nursing, drafting and model making, and electricity and computer/electronics.

Oak Park and River Forest, Illinois

Oak Park and River Forest are Chicago (residential) suburbs with a combined population of 70,000 and only one high school. River Forest, which sends less than 15 percent of the student population but owns 25 percent of the total assessed evaluation, is the wealthier of the two towns. Oak Park's population includes people at the poverty level as well as millionaires. The home and studio of Frank Lloyd Wright, who lived and worked in Oak Park for over 20 years, is only a few blocks from the school.

In the early years of the century, citizens of these two communities set out to create a strong school system so that even the richest families would send their children to the high school. To accomplish this goal, *Oak Park and River Forest High School* had to be good enough to get its graduates into the Eastern colleges and universities. This is still considered a measure of excellence. Of the 70 students from the Chicago area who applied to Princeton last year, seven were accepted. Four of them were from Oak Park and River Forest High School.

Under Superintendent M. R. McDaniel, one of the organizers of the National Honor Society, Oak Park and River Forest realized their dream. An outstanding faculty was recruited from a wide range of colleges and universities, and the "salary schedule was the highest in the Middle West. The requirements of performance were rigorous; however, there was no pressure upon teachers to go to summer school; rather, encouragement was given for travel and relaxation." [2] Years later, James Conant—President of Harvard and author of *The American High School Today,* the 1959 report that launched a major examination of the high school curriculum—praised Oak Park and River Forest High School as a "model of what a comprehensive high school should be." [3]

The area's biggest attraction is its excellent school system. "People in this town are in a state of school intoxication.... People stay pro-school because they remember how well their children—and their grandchildren, in many cases—did.... In this town people's hopes and aspirations for their children are tied up in the school."

The first unit of the present four-square block, 61 million dollar complex was opened in 1907. The large facility for over 3,000 students includes a 1,700-seat auditorium, a 450-seat small theater, a student theater that seats 100 (18 plays are presented each year), two swimming pools, eight gymnasiums, a dance studio, and, as we found in several other network schools, its own television facilities. The school has three bands and three orchestras and offers four years of Latin and two levels of calculus. The school library contains 60,000 books.

A respect for tradition is an important aspect of the school. Perhaps the most obvious symbol is the Oxford Room, which is decorated in English Tudor style with a fretted, beamed ceiling, wood paneling, a fireplace, and a lectern for the teacher. The room looks the same today as it did when Ernest Hemingway, one of Oak Park and River Forest's most famous graduates, studied English there. Today he is remembered by an annual essay award.

Teachers share the community's enthusiasm for the school. One teacher described it affectionately as "Heavenly High." Even though the school's enrollment has dropped from a high of 4,500 to the current 3,360, not one tenured teacher has been RIFed. Local early retirement incentives supplement a state program. The average teacher in the school has taught 16 years, 13 at Oak Park and River Forest. According to Associate Principal Donald Offerman, "We don't want too much new blood. We like a teacher who has been teaching for about six years. When we find someone really good we want to trap that person [into staying] here." Teachers are paid well; 50 percent are at the top of the salary schedule. Teachers are frequently asked to speak to civic groups. More than half the faculty live in the community.

Interestingly, the teachers hold no group affiliation with either the NEA or the AFT. There are no teacher contracts, but there is a Faculty Senate. When asked how many people might want a union, the steering committee members could only think of one person. "We get everything we need. Why do we need a union?"

The school works hard to keep strong ties with the community. Student/parent handbooks are mailed directly to the home, as is the Program of Studies, so that every parent can see what takes place and can get involved. Every classroom has a telephone so that teachers can call *out* to parents whenever needed. Special free performances of musicals are held for 800 senior citizens. The school is viewed as a community center in other ways, too.

The network's largest school is administered by a superintendent/principal, two associate principals, and 14 deans. The school has no guidance counselors; the deans counsel students and provide guidance. An alphabetical method of assigning students to deans for counseling allows students from the same family to share the same counselor. In an unusual departure, the deans are also responsible for disciplining their charges. "This system works for us because we know everything about our advisees." (Throughout the remaining chapters, Oak Park and River Forest High School will be referred to more briefly as "Oak Park.")

Page, Arizona

With a town population of about 5,000 and an area population of 15,000, Page is the smallest community with the smallest school (725 students) in the network. It is approximately 135 miles from Flagstaff (pop. 35,000) and 250 miles from Phoenix, the state capital. School officials described the town as "typical of small communities in the West; we are physically isolated from university and urban influences."

Although small in size, the key word to describe Page is "power." On its outskirts are the Glen Canyon Dam and the Navajo Generating Plant. The Glen Canyon Dam, one of the highest dams in the country, holds back 186-mile long Lake Powell, which is part of the Colorado River storage system. The Navajo Generating Plant, which gets its fuel from the rich deposits at Black Mesa, is the largest coal-fed generating plant in the western United States. Together these two facilities produce huge amounts of power for the West.

Page, which is both in and near some of the nation's most awesome natural scenery, began as a community to serve construction personnel and their families who were building the Glen Canyon Dam, which was completed in 1966. The city owns most of the available land and housing, which is even more expensive than in Phoenix. The entire school system is located in an educational park at one end of town.

Page High School plays a major role in community life. It has a young faculty, most of whom are in their 30s. The school facilities are impressively new and clean. A centrally located, carpeted, and upholstered "conversation pit" is a popular gathering place before school hours and between classes.

Anglo and Navajo cultures meet in this school. There are some racial problems but little violence. No teachers have ever been assaulted. The major problem for both Anglo and Navajo students alike is their low aspiration level. About 50 percent of the students were described as having high aspirations; the school and the community are attempting to raise the sights of the other half. The school places a strong emphasis on language, oral as well as written, since English is a second language for many Navajo youngsters.

The school boasts a strong vocational program. Graduates of the welding program can look forward to high-paying jobs at the Navajo

Generating Plant. The school's welding teacher, we were told by faculty members, eventually left his teaching job to join his students at the Navajo Generating Plant at a much higher salary. Then, displaying a rare dedication, he quit that job after a few months to return to his first love—*teaching!* To the teaching staff he is a true local hero.

Pinellas County, Florida

Pinellas Park High School is one of 14 high schools in Pinellas County, Florida, the twenty-third largest school system in the United States, and the fifth largest in Florida. Located on the Gulf Coast, Pinellas County is the most important tourist center on Florida's west coast.

The school, which opened in 1976, is the youngest in the network. Located in mid-county, it draws its diverse student body from five communities: Seminole, St. Petersburg, Clearwater, Pinellas Park, and Largo. Ninety-four percent of the students are transported by bus. There has been no overall decline in enrollment; in fact, this area is still growing.

When Pinellas Park High School first opened, many parents were reluctant to send their children to the new school, especially since many of their children would have attended Clearwater High School, which already enjoyed an excellent reputation. The new building principal and assistant principal handpicked the best department chairs they could find to assemble the new faculty; half were new to the system, and half transferred from other schools in the county. Assistant Principal Dorothy Cheathem, a key figure in the school's ASCD work, was selected as assistant principal for curriculum development, a responsibility that foreshadowed the school's intention to build a strong program. Over the last few years, these efforts have paid off. Pinellas Park was asked to represent the county in its bid for membership in the ASCD project and to use this opportunity to further strengthen its work.

The school, a very well-maintained building, is built around a huge central core where students keep their lockers and eat lunch. Radiating from this core are separate wings for the various subject-matter areas. As in other network schools, whenever any vandalism is done, the damage is repaired immediately to discourage any further such activity.

The school is proud of its unique Developmental Guidance Program. The program has its own curriculum at each grade level: Self and Career Awareness in the 9th grade; Decision Making in the 10th grade; Making Post-High School Plans in the 11th grade; and Implementing These Plans in the 12th grade. Students are "borrowed" from regular classes for one week so that this curriculum can be taught. The idea is to "generate business" in counseling rather than to wait for students to come to the counselors.

The students, who seemed genuinely proud of their school, made it a point to come to us on their own. They told us, "There are no integration problems here. We get along with one another." In spite of the school's intense pride in their first winning football season, there is a genuine attempt to balance the interest in academics and sports. School officials were also proud of the fact that many art teachers were practicing artists, a fact that we observed in other project schools.

San Rafael, California

San Rafael, California, a town of 45,000 people, is located in Marin County across the Golden Gate Bridge from San Francisco. Located in one of the nation's wealthier counties (the second highest median income in the country), San Rafael developed in the early 19th century as the village nearest to the Mission San Rafael. Gradually, the town and county became a resort area, which grew rapidly after the opening of the Golden Gate Bridge.

San Rafael differs in several respects from other communities in the county. It has a minority population of 14 percent in a county that is approximately 95 percent Anglo. Although there are very expensive houses in the town, rental homes are also available, which is unusual for Marin County. The availability of rental housing, plenty of low-paying jobs, and the good climate have attracted many multinational refugees to San Rafael. Thirty-two different languages are spoken in the San Rafael schools. In addition, the families of some of the inmates at San Quentin Prison live in the school district. Thus, San Rafael has students from both ends of the socioeconomic spectrum. About 50 percent of the work force commutes to San Francisco.

According to Superintendent Nancy Marley, for years *San Rafael High School* was considered to be "the" high school in the county. Although the county has always been fiercely pro-education, Proposition 13 has hurt San Rafael, as it has many other schools in the state. The weekly faculty bulletins, however, still exhort teachers to "stay with excellence."

In spite of the influx of people from other nations, San Rafael High School is suffering major enrollment declines. Teachers with as many as 16 years of experience have been RIFed; the average teacher's age is approximately 52. Most teachers are at the top of the salary schedule and live in the county, although not necessarily in San Rafael.

The school sends a high percentage of its students to college, over half to area junior colleges. The campus, which is closed while classes are in session, boasts a new music patio. All students take a 20-minute "brunch break" each mid-morning, during which they can eat a snack or meet outside with friends. There is a limited program in vocational education, but administrators feel that their program is good. A regional occupational program in "foods" is considered particularly excellent.

Scarsdale, New York

Located in Westchester County, north of New York City, Scarsdale is a community of 17,500 people. Its population—the epitome of the wealthy, suburban community—is made up mostly of business and professional people who enthusiastically support the public school system: only 10 percent of the children attend private schools; the rest attend the public schools.

The community's many Oriental families have helped maintain enrollments. Nevertheless, enrollments have declined by approximately 200 students in the last two years and will probably decline to 1,200 students by the end of the current decade.

School budgets pass every year in spite of the fact that the property tax is the main source of revenue (state support actually decreases each year because it remains the same in an inflationary economy). The town is not heavily indebted, and, surprisingly, its taxes are not the highest in the county. The Scarsdale schools spend their money prudently; for example, when a new high school auditorium budgeted at $1.5 million drew bids of $1.8 million, the school did not go back to the town for more money but, instead, cut back on plans for the addition. The school building is charming but not ostentatious. School officials work at economizing whenever possible.

Where they do not economize, however, is on teachers' salaries. Scarsdale teachers (we heard conflicting reports) are either the best paid or among the best paid teachers in the county. Scarsdale's commitment is to spend money to hire the best possible teachers. They look for candidates with four to five years of teaching experience. Department heads hold high levels of responsibility; they teach 60 percent of the time and spend 40 percent of their time on departmental responsibilities for which they receive extra pay. Each department has its own budget.

Like Oak Park and River Forest High School, *Scarsdale High School* was also cited by James Conant as being outstanding. It is a college preparatory high school, which last year sent one of every seven graduating seniors to an Ivy League institution. School administrators believe that this year's total of 37 National Merit finalists is the highest number achieved in 1984 by any school in the country. Although the school has three tracks, most students in all three tracks will go on to college. "There is a college somewhere for every student; every student takes the SATs," commented one counselor.

The curriculum includes Honors and Advanced Placement courses in all major academic areas. Students are given every chance for success. Tutorials are available in foreign languages for students who cannot keep up in class, and there are independent study programs and even a small Alternative School. Juniors and seniors are expected to do a research paper both years as part of their English requirements. Beyond the 9th grade there are no study halls, and the campus is open for juniors and seniors; it is simply assumed that students will behave.

Teacher morale is good. Scarsdale was described as a stable system. Faculty members are members of an AFT affiliate, which is a force in negotiations; however, we saw no example of an adversarial relationship between the faculty and the board or between the faculty and the administration. In fact, there hasn't been a single grievance in the past seven years.

Ventura, California

Buena and Ventura High Schools take their names from the Mission San Buenaventura, which was founded in 1782 on the site of a Chumäsh Indian settlement. Located 60 miles north of Los Angeles, Ventura is one of the oldest towns in California, with a population of approximately 75,000. It boasts beautiful beaches, serves as headquarters for the Channel Islands National Park, and is fast becoming a major tourist area. Ventura can best be described as an upwardly mobile bedroom community. At one time an important oil-producing area, Ventura has several active offshore oil platforms. The town sits on the Oxnard Plain, which has some of the best topsoil in the world. For example, California leads the nation in the production of 70 agricultural commodities, 26 of which are grown in Ventura. Ventura's population ranges from the very affluent to the very poor with a considerable contingent of transients, many of whom are oil workers, and growing proportions of Hispanics and retirees.

The two high schools, Buena and Ventura, serve somewhat varied populations within the community. Buena is on the side of town that is growing most rapidly as new tracts are built among shrinking agricultural plots. During the 1960s and 70s it sought less change than did Ventura High and was considered to be the more traditional of the two schools. With recent growth, it has had to face the problems that occur with an influx of students. Ventura, on the other hand, has had a student turnover rate as high as 40 percent because it serves a more transient population. Many townspeople and school personnel had grown tired of the proliferation of courses and the open campus atmosphere and wanted to see a tightening of requirements.

It became obvious to district level administrators that something needed to be done to redefine and strengthen the programs at both schools and to tighten up programs and graduation requirements for all students. Many of the teachers we interviewed credit two men— Assistant Superintendent for Instruction Jack Partin (a former principal of Ventura High) and Director of Secondary Education John Bay—with persuading the two schools to join the ASCD project.

Both schools have campuses that include several one-story buildings, courtyards, patios, extensive lawns and ground covers, swimming pools, and large bicycle park areas. The principals—Mike

Shanahan at Buena and Bob Cousar at Ventura—were formerly assistant principals at *each other's* schools, an arrangement that gives both an unusual understanding and appreciation for the job his colleague faces. This relationship appeared to give the two schools an advantage when they came together to negotiate a common stance based on what they had done separately.

Taken either singly or collectively this is a fascinating group of schools. Each has a unique identity and distinct set of problems, and each reflects a different social milieu. As the network process of redefining general education in the American high school began, questions arose. "How will each school organize to conduct the process?" "What will each school accomplish?" The first task that each school faced after the initial network meeting in Racine, Wisconsin, was to organize a process for conducting the study.

3 The Process

The speakers were exciting, thought-provoking . . . they challenged us to think beyond our day-to-day problems.

The participants from the original network meetings still felt this inspiration and excitement three years later, as we confirmed again and again in each of our visits. Although some representatives from smaller schools confessed that they initially felt uneasy about "being in the same league with some of those big-city schools" or some of those like Scarsdale, for example, that were on somebody's "ten best list," once the initial conference got under way, all fears faded as participants threw themselves into the issue at hand—the redefinition of general education.

In retrospect, several schools wished that they could have sent more people to those initial meetings because transmitting that initial enthusiasm to the teachers and opinion molders who hadn't been there wasn't easy. Ames Principal Ralph Farrar said that if he had to do it all over again, he would have taken his steering committee and all the department heads at Ames High School on a local retreat and organized it so that these leaders could have been inspired as he had been. Predictably, as soon as it was financially feasible, districts fashioned their own at-home versions of the first network meeting. For example, Baltimore, Denver, Ventura, and others showed their committees the ASCD videotape, *Redefining General Education in the American High School,* in which Boyer, Cawelti, and Broudy discussed the concept of general education. Baltimore would eventually see to it that several of its faculty would hear firsthand such educational leaders as Ernest Boyer, Jane Stallings, Allan Glatthorn, and ASCD Past President Lucille Jordan. Admittedly, telling people about what had happened was a pale substitute; still, it was better than nothing at all. At least one teacher hesitated to do even this with his colleagues because they might ask why *he* had been chosen in the first place.

Getting Started

Once the various delegations returned home, the first order of business was to organize the redefinition process. Without exception, the first step was to install a committee or task force. In Ventura and Ann Arbor with two schools each, districtwide committees were selected. The same was true in San Rafael where a second high school not part of the ASCD network was included. Declining enrollments will probably lead to consolidation within the next three years; hence, it seemed logical to begin joint planning immediately.

Woodlawn Senior High School in Baltimore County had its own "Dimensions" steering committee, which worked jointly with the county senior high committee so that all 21 county high schools could benefit from the work at Woodlawn. According to the county's central administration, Woodlawn was selected as Baltimore County's representative because its 1,900 students represented a microcosm of the area's population. Woodlawn is also thought of as a typical Baltimore County comprehensive high school. The other large systems in the network—New Orleans, Pinellas County, and Denver—will also eventually report to the central administration and/or the other high schools in their community as well, but they are not part of such a concerted effort as in Baltimore County.

The sizes of task forces and steering committees varied considerably. New Orleans' steering committee had four faculty members who, in turn, formed several subcommittees when needed. Ventura High School's committee consisted of the principal and representatives from the school's five divisions. At the other end of the continuum, Buena High School (located in Ventura) established a volunteer school committee of 23 members. Ames instituted three leadership structures:

1. A steering committee of seven teachers, the principal, the associate superintendent for curriculum and instruction, a member of the

board of education, and one person from an area educational service unit.

2. Eight mixed interdepartmental groups of ten members, each of which was formed to cross departmental lines and increase communication.

3. Traditional department coordinators who, with steering committee help, acted as an additional liaison to the staff.

Committee Selection and Membership

The membership of these committees also varied considerably. Every committee included classroom teachers, and all but one committee included a building administrator. Five committees, including the single high school districts of Ames and Scarsdale, invited a district level administrator to serve. Four districts included students on their steering committees, five included parents, and three added board members to the group. Curiously, not one district included members from *all* these groups, even though the literature eloquently pleads for the involvement of each, without whose cooperation change is seen as an impossibility.

From our interviews in the schools, it is difficult to say which of these groups should ideally be represented on a committee. Schools that included students reported that they made an important contribution. The teenagers' point of view was informative and realistic. One major drawback with including students was that most of them graduated before the process was finished, and replacing them was difficult. Involving parents also presented a problem; in some cases the parents were neither very active nor very helpful. On the other hand, one Denver mother of six was considered a "school treasure." An ardent supporter of East High, she articulated as clearly as anyone could the issues that the school faced. Several teachers told us, "Listen to *her*; she knows what needs to be done."

Reviews were mixed when it came to adding board members to the building committees. Most schools felt that this was unnecessary since local boards of education would eventually hear what had been done anyway. The three districts that did add board members to their committees did so because they wanted the board to be aware firsthand of what was going on. This did not work very well in one case because the board member had her own ax to grind. In Oak Park, on the other hand, the committee was fortunate to have a board member who was unusually articulate, thought-provoking, and helpful. As a building administrator put it, "If every school board had a Leah Marcus, American education would be way ahead of where it is now!"

In retrospect, most of the individuals responsible for organizing the school committees did not regret their choices of the *groups* that they included. About organizing the committee, we frequently heard the laments, "We didn't get the 'right' teachers involved," "We didn't get enough opinion leaders on the committee," or "You must have the power brokers [on the committee], the people that other teachers will listen to and follow." This, obviously, was a critical factor; if the movers and shakers weren't involved, committees had a tougher time getting things done.

In most cases volunteer committees did not work as well as committees that were formulated to include key decision groups or departments/divisions that had the most or least to gain. Nevertheless, in one case the administrator reported that he had no choice but to go with volunteers because of the way the union contract was written. Volunteers from *within* the major power groups were more effective than random volunteers from the faculty. All agreed that the best arrangement was a committee that included active people who would speak their minds and who would work to accomplish something. In several cases the principal recruited these people.

However, recruiting committee members did not mean stacking the deck so that the committee would come up with what the principal or other administrator wanted. In the privacy of the interview some teachers, even after three years of involvement, wondered what the administration's hidden agenda really was. Few in the schools today would accept Dickens' lines, "It was the best of times . . . it was the age of wisdom," although many might suspect that "it was the worst of times . . . the season of Darkness."[1] Certainly, it is an age of RIFs, tax cuts or tax binds, and challenges to education from every possible direction. Teachers who fear school closings, school consolidation, budget cutbacks, program elimination, and requests for more work (with little or no accompanying pay) are bound to be skeptical about the real reason for involvement in an activity such as the ASCD network.

Initial Skepticism

The skepticism we saw was usually caution about whether all the work was "busy work" to make the administration and/or the district look good. Nevertheless, the question of motive was an important issue at only two network sites. In both cases there had been one or more major administrative turnovers at the building and/or district levels and/or a board of education turnover. In these towns we heard the following comments:

> This new board is going to run the district and will tell the superintendent what it wants done. They are very political.

> The administrator is a good guy, but he's really only a figurehead.

> These administrators are nothing but pawns of the board. They will do only what the board wants done.

> This is an excuse for a back-to-basics movement.

> They want to get rid of one of our best courses because it isn't taught in the other high schools.

> This administration wants to set a personal agenda.

> The administrator doesn't even know what's going on.

Even in those buildings where these suspicions seemed widespread, other faculty members did not share them:

> His goal is to get people to think about curriculum. We realize that someone has to stir things up if we're going to move forward.

In general, I don't believe there was much in the way of hidden agendas. Having seen more than one classroom spruced up for visiting dignitaries, I looked for Potemkin Villages.[2] I didn't find any. What I found was that most administrators sincerely wanted the chance to fulfill the ASCD mission. A few administrators did believe their faculties were change-resistant and that the only way to get things moving was to shake the foundations, to provoke teachers into a course of action. Whatever their method, however, their goals were the same: *self-examination* and *redefinition*. Granted, in some cases, this self-examination fit in neatly with an upcoming school accreditation, so the ASCD charge was a good way to begin something that needed to be done anyway. Thus, more often than not, the districts in the network had already begun a process of self-examination; ASCD served as a catalyst to focus on, heighten, or continue that process.

For example, Pioneer High School had won a grant a few years ago to help develop the teaching of the humanities. This grant was seen as a way to integrate learning—to end the egg-crate separation of knowledge:

> ASCD gave us the chance to think through the implications of this work for all youngsters. What are the different ways of seeing and hearing? In what ways can we make art more than something to cover a hole in the wall?

Teachers on the Steering Committees

Teachers who agreed to serve on steering committees did so for a variety of reasons. Many had listened to a detailed description of what the charge was and what was planned and were eager to get involved; in some cases, the faculty had actually voted to join the network. Pinellas Park High School in Largo, Florida, and Oak Park and River Forest High School in Illinois had applied to be part of the network because they were continually trying to update their programs. As several people noted when we were in Oak Park, nobody in the community was particularly surprised when *A Nation at Risk* and the other national reports burst on the national scene; their high schools had already been involved in a serious self-examination for over two years. That was the way things were done in Oak Park; it was a tradition to be on the cutting edge. Further, it was only natural that teachers would be willing to volunteer to serve.

We frequently heard that this was a chance "to look at education for kids in the middle." There was considerable agreement that special education had come a long way and that the bright students probably were going to go far beyond any minimum that might be defined. (As the process unfolded, we observed this was in no way a unanimous belief.) But what about the youngsters in the middle? Teachers felt these students weren't being challenged enough; all too often they were left alone because they didn't demand much and they didn't make any trouble. Some teachers were hoping changes in graduation requirements would help these students.

Some teachers were eager to be involved in a project where they would have the chance to rub shoulders with faculty members from schools in other parts of the country. Other teachers joined because they wanted to make sure their territories or beliefs did not get lost in the shuffle. What was going to happen to industrial arts? To physical education? Counselors wanted to ensure that the affective domain would not be ignored. Teachers from several disciplines wanted their students to learn "life skills as well as the basics." Several joined because they saw the need to work with colleagues in other high schools in their districts. Still others were willing to serve on a steering committee because they had faith in their building administrators.

The Process Unfolds

Although the processes that the network schools used varied along significant lines, important common denominators emerged.

In districts with several high schools, involvement with the larger body of schools always existed. In Denver, principals and curriculum supervisors held citywide meetings, while in New Orleans curriculum specialists from the central administration took part in the school's activities. In Pinellas County, the county secondary curriculum committee—composed of teachers, students, parents, supervisors, and administrators—was kept informed as were the people on the school curriculum committee and the parents' advisory committee.

Woodlawn High School, as noted earlier, was part of an elaborate structure that embraced all 21 high schools in Baltimore County. Their process was by far the most elaborate of those in the large systems. At the county level, for example, there were study committees that dealt with: the grouping of students, scheduling pupil information, diplomas, testing, attendance, staffing, grading and promotion practices, support services, waivers/released time, work study, graduation requirements, transition to work/post-secondary, and the Middle States Evaluation of High Schools. Woodlawn's task/study groups could both draw from and add to these groups.

Strong Beginnings

Leaders in the network schools felt strongly that how the project was initiated had a lot to do with how successful it was in the long run. [3]

Many now agree that there is a critical need to define the task and explain the reasons why it is being undertaken. In Page, in the two Ventura schools, in Baltimore County, in Ames, and in Oak Park, the steering committees began by defining general education. In schools where this was never done clearly, teachers said that the project suffered. In at least two instances schools felt that ASCD should have given them more direction in putting together a definition. The real issue, however, wasn't as much a matter of definition as it was having some sense of the vastness of the scope of the project. Since everyone was new to the process and there weren't any predetermined guidelines, defining the scope was difficult.

Once their committees were organized, several schools held orientation meetings. Pioneer and Huron High Schools held sessions for the board of education, the two faculties, parents, and (uniquely) students. In Ames, department coordinators held a series of meetings.

As might be expected, the steering committees in all the schools met frequently. Some members did a lot of research. As we will see later, one of the most important publications that many schools used was a draft of the College Board publication, *Academic Preparation for College — What Students Need To Know and Be Able To Do,* which was published in 1983. The Oak Park committee brought in speakers. In San Rafael, each committee member was asked to design an ideal curriculum so that it could be shared with and examined by the rest of the committee. In Oak Park, the steering committee listed the experiences necessary to meet the terms of its definition of general education. In Pinellas Park, the committee met biweekly to write down the concepts and skills that it thought were important. In the intervening weeks the three committee members who had attended the network meeting summarized and organized the committee's ideas under broad headings. These were presented to the entire committee when it returned for its next meeting. At this time, committee members were asked to list more specific concepts under the broad headings. This process allowed for review and modification throughout the process.

In Carlsbad, the committee worked both as a whole and as subcommittees. In Scarsdale, the committee asked two questions: What skills and knowledge should students acquire before they graduate? What courses should be required in order to help students acquire these skills and this knowledge? To help answer these questions, the committee reviewed graduation requirements, discussed with the departments their course offerings, and looked at the pattern of course selection made by the class of 1981. Carlsbad did much the same thing. They studied 111 transcripts selected randomly from the 430 members of the 1981 graduating class. The desired balance across four major subject areas—the arts, math/science/technology, family/leisure/health, and citizenship/societal information—was present by and large; nevertheless, many college-bound students were not taking the courses recommended for college preparation, particularly in math and science. This finding fit in with the concerns raised by many national reports. The ASCD study spotlighted what had happened in that particular school.

In certain schools the process remained in the hands of the committee; in others, the steering committees eventually turned more frequently to the faculty for help. Page asked the faculty which concepts and skills should be taught. Ames formed eight groups of ten teachers; each group represented several departments so that the lines of communication would be open.

San Rafael's faculty members were asked to address two questions: What *is* and what *should be?* These questions served as a discrepancy model so that the faculty could get at the issue of "What is really in the best interest of our kids?" In doing this the committee down-played the fact that they were part of an ASCD project, with the emphasis on "our needs." Eventually the committee/faculty deliberations led to discussion of four proposals to make changes in graduation requirements. Upon hearing of the work going on in San Rafael, the California state legislature called on Principal Steve Collins to testify at one of its hearings.

Some schools sought involvement via a large cross section of the faculty. In Ann Arbor, student representatives, parent groups, and the faculties of Pioneer and Huron were all asked to brainstorm and suggest common learnings, from which the two faculties created a list of common learnings to send the steering committee.

Pinellas Park and O. Perry Walker faculties both established released time (two afternoons and three days respectively) in order to get their faculties involved. O. Perry Walker arranged teachers' visits to see what other schools were doing, a tried and true method for bringing about change. Pinellas Park added a staff development component to the released time so that the staff could earn inservice credit. The faculty was divided into 12 cross-disciplinary groups so they could discuss the steering committee's proposals. Later these same teachers met at the departmental level. Meetings of this type were frequent in most network schools. The quality of the response varied from school to school.

Faculty members sometimes looked upon the discussions as "busy work" with a blasé comment, "We've done this before, and nothing happened." One memorable comment centered on the periodic swings of the educational pendulum, "Don't change anything. Once every 15 years you're going to be right." A few people thought that the discussions raised unnecessary stress. In Ventura, a number of people were genuinely pleased that the meetings were "real eye openers" for all involved.

No other school took as strong a stance on the importance of the process as did Ventura. Ventura took the position that "it is the *process* that will truly determine action, not the document itself." The committee's job was first to help teachers perceive that there *was* a need; next to free the faculty's "creative energies"; and finally, to assist teachers in reaching a consensus. The leadership assumed that change by its very nature implied upheaval; hence, the greater the change, the greater the upheaval.

> That means that there will be argument, anger, frustration, a tearing apart. . . . Let it happen and let it happen early. Also, the more people involved in this process, the better. Managers might not reach the ends they want, but they should have the vision to see "structure and outline" and be flexible about content. Consensus takes time, but the more people who share in the planning, the more who are committed to a plan's success.

The Importance of Faculty Discussion

In spite of a few skeptics, the overwhelming majority of people we interviewed were enthusiastic about the faculty discussions that took place throughout the process. Whether they were looking at definitions, writing self-evaluations, or discussing and arguing about concepts, skills, or courses, teachers and administrators obviously enjoyed talking with one another. It didn't seem to make any difference *when* this was done during the process; the important thing was that it was done.

This self-examination gets you thinking about what you are doing.

It helps us to rediscover things that we don't ordinarily think about in our day-to-day activities.

For the first time we talked about what's in the best interest of the kids.

It wasn't like all these national reports; it wasn't "what's wrong with us?" but "what are we going to do in the future?"

Even though we questioned them two or more years later, teachers described these discussions with enthusiasm, indeed with fondness. People seemed to agree that everyone who wanted to have input had a chance. The only regret in most schools was that the feelings generated by these discussions hadn't lasted.

Teachers felt that sharing with their colleagues gave them a global view, resulting in less fragmentation of knowledge and less teacher isolation. An industrial arts teacher in Denver reported with delight that after a meeting an English teacher actually talked to him about technical writing. Another English teacher was amazed to discover that several vocational education teachers took points off for spelling: "I wasn't the only one who was trying to improve writing skills! I thought I was fighting that battle all by myself."

At first, the discussions tended to be utopian, "We had a heck of a time getting folks off the ideal to talk about specifics!" People had to express their feelings about what the curriculum should be. It took a lot of time, but it was an important part of the process. "We have a lot of good teachers whose ideas don't get recognized."

In hindsight, several schools wished that they could have done more to capitalize on this early involvement and enthusiasm. Ventura Principal Bob Cousar saw that involving people ended the pessimistic attitude, "Leave me alone in my classroom. Nothing's going to change." Consciousness had been raised. Ventura High School's final report stated that although the involvement step took time, it paid off in the long run because it prompted people to get involved in the planning. When this happened, more teachers were committed to success; the burden fell less heavily on the school and on project leadership. We will explore this theme in Chapter 5.

Principal Ron Barnes has seen to it that Scarsdale has built on their faculty discussions. Even though the project is officially over, time is now devoted in regular faculty meetings to discussion of what is going on in the various departments and what new things they are trying to do.

Innovative Techniques

Faculty discussions were not the only method used in developing a process. Several schools used a variety of techniques that would give them information *and* get people involved. Questionnaires were distributed to students and teachers at various stages. O. Perry Walker developed a formal needs assessment, which student teams took into local shopping centers to collect community attitudes and opinions.

All-day workshops were common, but Baltimore, for instance, also held a summer workshop in which teachers and administrators developed an achievement certificate to serve as an adjunct to the Maryland High School Diploma. The participants were paid per diem for their work.

Surprisingly, few districts used long-term outside consultants, such as local college and university faculty. O. Perry Walker did use consultants from Tulane University and the University of New Orleans to assist with workshop activities.

Interim oral and written reports to the faculty were common, as were reports to boards of education and to curriculum coordinators in the system. Eventually recommendations were made to faculties, administrations, boards, and PTA's.

Scarsdale used a technique that no other school used. Principal Ron Barnes and Assistant Principal Corwith Hansen drew up a set of subject-free questions, which they asked faculty in each department to respond to in writing (see Figure 5). Responses were then sent to outside consultants for evaluation. The backgrounds of outside consultants were quite varied. Some were department chairs from other high schools, some were from the community, and others were college professors.

The consultants' evaluation reports were then given to the departments. Faculty members occasionally were "uptight" about being evaluated by unknown people, especially people from the commu-

Figure 5. Scarsdale High School's Graduation Requirements Committee
Questionnaire

1. What are the skills and knowledge areas, organized by grade, that the
   department teaches? At what grade level does the major emphasis occur?

2. What are the priorities among the skills and knowledge now being taught?

3. Is a written syllabus available for each course? If so, please include it.

4. What skills and topics would the department like to teach that it is not now
   teaching?

5. Should more or fewer years of the discipline be required for graduation?

6. What social, economic, and technological trends does the department
   perceive will affect the future of its teaching? What changes does the
   department anticipate in response to these trends?

7. How does the department define the distinctive characteristic(s) of its
   discipline in relationship to other disciplines? How is this conveyed to
   students?

8. What skills and topics are important for the discipline that are not taught
   within the department because teachers assume they are taught in another
   department? For example, do math and science teachers teach the special
   reading necessary to their discipline?

nity. Some felt that the evaluators did not understand the reports, were
uninformed or had a personal ax to grind. However, others found a
specific report thought-provoking and of major help in a departmental
self-examination. These high-powered reports raised fundamental
issues, some of which the faculty feel still need to be addressed.

To get faculty involved the Oak Park and River Forest committees
tried a number of practices that were common to the other schools as
well. Associate Principal Don Offerman and the steering committee
made presentations during an inservice day, as did a dean from the
University of Chicago who helped point out issues to be considered.
There were bulletins, memoranda, a survey (the results of which were
later published) and, inevitably, faculty discussions. To organize for
these discussions, the faculty was divided into quartiles by length of
teaching experience. The various discussion groups were then set up

as mixtures of the four groups. Mixing the "old pros" and the younger teachers was important if a real sense of community was to be maintained.

It was inevitable that there would be peaks and valleys in enthusiasm for the process, "You've got to keep things stirred up so that everyone knows something is happening." Revitalization was necessary for committees and faculties alike. Don Offerman expressed the belief that enthusiasm can be kept alive by varying the approach. In Oak Park, this might mean hiring substitute teachers for a day so that the committee could be free to continue its work. After donating their own time, teachers appreciated being taken out by the administration for a leisurely meal. The O. Perry Walker faculty had breakfast together, which was a friendly way to start the morning before beginning their all-day workshops. "Show them that their work is appreciated. Give them the chance to go to conferences that might enhance what they are doing," said the administrators.

The Need for Compromise

Sometimes you just have to compromise. As a school administrator or committee leader or member, you may never get *all* that you think you want, but if you can modify your hopes, you are likely to get *most* of what you want.

Don Offerman, a key figure in Oak Park, said that there is only so much that a committee can do; eventually there has to be some "personal politicking." He went to every department at least once and sometimes as many as three times to talk with faculty members. In some cases it was a matter of going "one on one" to show people what the project was trying to do.

Somebody has to take the ball and run with it. You can't concede on all points, but you do have to take other people's ideas into account. If nothing else, you get to know the people in your building a lot better!

Perhaps the best example of compromise at work occurred in the two Ann Arbor schools, Pioneer and Huron. Ann Arbor, according to many people in the district, was a city that had felt more than its share of the turmoil of the 1960s and 1970s. Many issues, such as racial problems and bitter feelings about the war in Vietnam, spilled over into the schools. There had been many changes, much diversity in the schools. Some innovations had been tried and were very unpopular; frequently the tension was high. Many people saw the ASCD project as a convenient opportunity not only to redefine general education in the high schools, but also to refocus the mission of high schools. As a result, during the first year of the project, enormous effort went into discussing common learnings. First, both Pioneer and Huron came up with their own lists. Then, people from the two-schools drew up a common list of proposed learnings, which the steering committee hoped to circulate throughout the community.

At this point deliberations disintegrated. The board of education believed that the teachers were moving too slowly; the teachers thought they were being pushed too fast. The board wanted results before its term ended (by *results* they meant changes in graduation requirements). In no small part, people thought this rush was caused by nationally published reports, such as *A Nation at Risk,* which started appearing in the spring of 1983. On the other hand, the teachers did not want to lose ownership in a project in which they had invested so much effort. When the administration was directed to speed up its efforts, the proceedings became adversarial; and teacher enthusiasm waned dramatically. Many teachers felt the board did not trust them.

During the summer and into September 1983, several changes took place. The superintendent retired, a new board was elected, and a bitter dispute arose over contract negotiations. The dispute led to a 16-day strike at the start of the 1983-1984 school year. The prospects looked dim for continuing the ASCD project. Many teachers we interviewed thought that they had lost control of the process and that any results would come "from the top down." Much suspicion centered on a 72-page document, "Proposals for High School Program Improvement," which included the work done in the two schools and the efforts of the steering committee. It had been put together for release in September 1983 by Acting Associate Superintendent for Curriculum and Instruction Richard Stock (then Director of Secondary Education), and Acting Superintendent Lee Hansen (then Associate Superintendent). Many people saw this green booklet (irreverently called the S&H Green Book) as a *fait accompli:* "The process was over, and it was out of our hands."

It was at this point that we drove into Ann Arbor to begin the interviews. We knew nothing of the conflict, but we soon heard both sides of the story. It was obvious that the staff, administration, and board of education believed in the process and wanted to continue with it but that it would have been fruitless to continue on the path they were on. Coincidentally, while we were visiting Ann Arbor, all parties agreed to meet in committee to set up a new timeline and create a format for completing the process that could be presented to both faculties for a vote. Shortly before we left Ann Arbor, the faculties voted overwhelmingly to support the new timetable. The steering committee's statement of common learnings will be the starting point. A 43-member high school curriculum task force—made up of students and graduates, faculty, administrators, parents, community representatives, minority group members, and others—will see to it that the common learnings are shared with the various professional and community groups in Ann Arbor to elicit their reactions.

The task force's final recommendations for common learnings will be presented to the board of education. Once the board has adopted these common learnings, a professional study committee made up of ten high school faculty members from the three Ann Arbor high schools, a building administrator from each of these high schools, and two intermediate school faculty members will compare the present curriculum with the adopted common learnings. After this is done, the committee will develop a draft proposal for graduation requirements, which will be reviewed by all groups represented on the task force.

Town meetings will be held so that anyone can voice an opinion about the proposal as it is debated and amended before it is finally given to the board of education along with recommendations from the administration for final action. The goal is to complete this process by early 1985.

The project is certainly alive again; all believe it will now be seen through to a successful conclusion. Some teachers told us that they thought people would get involved again because they want to finish what they had started. Others thought that, given what they had gone through, this time people might be even *more* serious about the process than ever before. Ann Arbor is to be congratulated. We were impressed at people's willingness to come together, compromise, and rectify what had earlier seemed a virtually hopeless situation.

Ownership and Leadership

In Ann Arbor, the ownership of the redefinition process appeared to have a rather broad base. It may seem contradictory, given what has been said so far, but this was not the case in many schools. *All* schools witnessed a high level of involvement by a large part of the faculty at one time or another during the process. More often than not, this occurred early in the process when everyone got together to talk about what should be, what was needed, and what might be done. In many schools this process continued as faculty discussed graduation requirements, common learnings, or other matters. Sometimes this involved the faculty as a whole; sometimes it was done in departments.

Broad faculty involvement was difficult to sustain over three years, so it fell to a critical mass of people to keep the process going. Every school had its low points, and a few endured the added burden of how to orient large numbers of new teachers who were the result of staff turnovers or school consolidations. By the end of the three-year process, unless there had been continuing involvement, faculties felt little sense of ownership. In certain instances many faculty members were not even aware of what was going on. Reported estimates of faculty ownership in each school ranged from 2% to 75% of faculty who knew what was going on in the redefinition process. We heard variations on the statement, "One third really know what is happening, one third have a vague idea, and the last third have no idea at all. It's a normal curve."

In nearly every case, long-term ownership rested mainly with the steering committee and one or more school administrators. In one exception the townwide steering committee was described as a "clearing committee" for content area subcommittees. By and large most of the committee members were very proud to have participated. A few people dropped out of committees; nevertheless, most committee members felt that they personally got a lot out of their work, even if everything had not worked out as well as they had initially hoped. The following comments were typical of the range we found:

> At first it didn't really hit home that we were really going to change, to actually do something!

> Once I saw what was involved in all this, I went out and enrolled in a curriculum course!

> For those people who really got involved, it was quite an eye opener. Here was a chance to do more than just complain. We saw new horizons.

> In general, the committee feels the faculty has bought in. Everyone who wanted it had input. Some just aren't aware, and they won't change. Inertia rules.

> Our committee took a lot of leadership. We opened windows for teachers and helped them get in touch with new ideas.

> How do you get people to *stay* involved?

Many people speculated on the size of the critical mass that was needed to keep a process working. With the committee and key administrators as the nucleus, how many people did you need on that committee? How many additional people did you need? We asked these questions in all the schools.

We found no consistent answer to these questions. The modal answer was a core of 15 to 20 people. What was really important was leadership.

Leadership involved system and building leaders. In Ames, Baltimore, and Ann Arbor, central office administrators played a crucial role in their district's project throughout its life. As might be expected, in a number of towns the building principal was *a* or *the* key actor.

This was not always the case, however. In five towns an assistant principal or dean of students was the *de facto* leader. Either these individuals were the author or co-authors of the original proposals, or they had been assigned later to the task. In some cases where the original co-author had been a principal who had subsequently left the district, his or her replacement felt awkward about stepping into a process that had "belonged" to someone else.

A few principals candidly admitted that the literature calls the principal "the instructional leader" in a school; but as one principal vividly expressed it, "This may be the greatest myth in American education today. What principal has the time to do all that should be done?" In fact, we met two principals who seemed to have very little knowledge at all about what was going on.

Principals Paul Rosier and Michael Shanahan at Page and Buena High Schools told us that they believed in the concept of shared leadership.[4] Rosier, who had been assistant principal when the project began, thought that the best way to get teachers involved in curriculum development was to step aside and let faculty members run the show, let them take the leadership and share the decision making, and support them at every step of the way. Shanahan believed that sharing leadership was a big confidence builder for the staff. He thought that Buena High School could not have made progress without this sharing. Both men, however, were very well informed and involved in the processes that unfolded in their schools.

In a few schools department heads played an important role, and in others they did not. We saw no discernible pattern. Our educated guess is that the role of department heads was not clearly defined. Further, it did not seem to make any difference if a school was a strong union or a strong nonunion school.

The trust that a faculty had in a principal was identified as a process advantage in some schools. We heard comments about principals being "strong, but fair," or "we can give him hell and he'll listen, and we won't be punished." This helps morale; and a few faculties even described their relationship as "like a family." However, we do not have enough evidence to conclude that this made a crucial difference in a project's final results. There were too many variables that could, and did, offset this feeling of trust.

One school voiced a caution about committee ownership/leadership. A committee may easily think through the ideas that a faculty will eventually come up with long before the faculty has a chance to hold its discussions. If the committee gives the impression that "we already had that idea," then the faculty members will feel rejected. A faculty also won't "buy in" if it appears that the committee is being manipulated by an administrator or that a committee isn't being given the chance to fully develop its thinking. One group said there was little freedom for anyone because the whole process was, as a participant put it, "city-directed."

Emergent Leadership

One of our most noteworthy findings in many schools was the rise of new leaders from the committee. They were the spark plugs who got things going and later got things done. They organized meetings, conducted workshops, cleared pathways. Some wrote the philosophies; others wrote the final reports. They did whatever it took to keep the process alive. We saw several examples of this. When we first entered Buena High School, we were told we had to meet Judy Bysshe because of the job she had done; across town at Ventura High School we were told to meet Lenore Crow. In Page, Arizona, it was Chuck Howells. It was Doug Lynn in Carlsbad, Ethel Istre and Merry Pawlowski in New Orleans, to name only a few of the new leaders who had emerged as a result of the project. "Having a classroom teacher in a key leadership position gave the whole project credibility," we were told. Since then several have gone into administration, most as assistant principals.

Selecting a Model

Once the project schools had decided upon their organizational framework, they moved to choose a curriculum model on which they could base their work. It was here that ASCD was especially helpful. The people who had attended the first Wingspread Conference in July 1981 and a follow-up conference seven months later were exposed to the thinking of educational leaders whose ideas would eventually make front page headlines in the second half of 1983 and in early 1984. These conferences were more than food for thought; they were a banquet, a veritable smorgasbord of ideas and concepts. The attendees were—in a word—"inspired."

Transmitting this inspiration to the faculty back home was not always easy, but the project leaders tried: they gave reports, showed the ASCD videotape, *Redefining General Education in the American High School,* and brought in their own follow-up speakers.

It was at this point, before moving to a model, that some schools decided that they should create their own definition of general education. A few schools would later incorporate these definitions into a newly written school philosophy. Representative examples of these definitions include:

Oak Park and River Forest: . . . general education by definition is that set of learning experiences all students must have.

Buena and Ventura: General education is the common learning experiences appropriate for all American youth.

Page: The general education component of the Page High School curriculum is composed of the concepts, ideas, skills, and experiences that *all* students will be exposed to. These common learnings form the foundation for students to become educated.

Woodlawn: General education is that aspect of a student's development that prepares him or her for a successful transition into the post-secondary school phase of living—the world of work or the continuation of formalized schooling. General education deals with a commonality of learning and experiences that enable all students to become adequately prepared to live productively, effectively, and humanely in the coming years.

Ames: Interdependence is the basic reality of human experience and the organizing principle of general education. The interdependence of skills and content is the central concept of a general education curriculum. Guided by this concept, a program of general education provides a foundation for continuous learning and conveys shared knowledge and experience common to all persons. The program focuses on the human experiences that enable students to live in harmony with themselves, and to be responsive to each other and to their several environments without endangering the preservation of a free society.

Although each definition has points in common with the others, each is also unique. How a school or community defines general education helps to determine its future direction.

In selecting a model, the schools went in several directions. The Boyer model (Figure 2, p. 9) was used exclusively by Pioneer and Huron, and by Denver's East High School. These schools believed that they could accomplish their goals by incorporating the Boyer model "with modifications" into their existing curriculum. Pinellas Park and O. Perry Walker used the Cawelti model (Figure 1, p. 8).

Scarsdale also decided to use a single model, the College Board's Basic Academic Competencies (Figure 6). Two earlier committees—one on graduation requirements, the other on the school's environment—had also been important influences.

Three districts combined aspects of the major models. The basic model of a balanced curriculum selected by Oak Park was Boyer's model (Figure 2) with modifications drawn from the Cawelti model (Figure 1). Page's steering committee looked at the

Figure 6. Basic Academic Competencies Defined by The College Board*

Reading

- The ability to identify and comprehend the main and subordinate ideas in a written work and to summarize the ideas in one's own words.
- The ability to recognize different purposes and methods of writing, to identify a writer's point of view and tone, and to interpret a writer's meaning inferentially as well as literally.
- The ability to separate one's personal opinions and assumptions from a writer's.
- The ability to vary one's reading speed and method (survey, skim, review, question, and master) according to the type of material and one's purpose for reading.
- The ability to use the features of books and other reference materials such as table of contents, preface, introduction, titles and subtitles, index, glossary, appendix, bibliography.
- The ability to define unfamiliar words by decoding, using contextual clues, or by using a dictionary.

Writing

- The ability to conceive ideas about a topic for the purpose of writing.
- The ability to organize, select, and relate ideas and to outline and develop them in coherent paragraphs.
- The ability to write Standard English sentences with correct:
  —Sentence structure.
  —Verb forms.
  —Punctuation, capitalization, possessives, plural forms, and other matters of mechanics.
  —Word choice and spelling.
- The ability to vary one's writing style, including vocabulary and sentence structure, for different readers and purposes.
- The ability to improve one's own writing by restructuring, correcting errors, and rewriting.
- The ability to gather information from primary and secondary sources; to write a report using this research; to quote, paraphrase, and summarize accurately; and to cite sources properly.

Academic Preparation For College: What Students Need To Know And Be Able To Do (New York: The College Board, 1983), pp. 7-10. Copyright 1983 by College Entrance Examination Board. All rights reserved.

Speaking and Listening

- The ability to engage critically and constructively in the exchange of ideas, particularly during class discussions and conferences with instructors.
- The ability to answer and ask questions coherently and concisely, and to follow spoken instructions.
- The ability to identify and comprehend the main and subordinate ideas in lectures and discussions, and to report accurately what others have said.
- The ability to conceive and develop ideas about a topic for the purpose of speaking to a group; to choose and organize related ideas; to present them clearly in Standard English; and to evaluate similar presentations by others.
- The ability to vary one's use of spoken language to suit different situations.

Mathematics

- The ability to perform, with reasonable accuracy, the computations of addition, subtraction, multiplication, and division using natural numbers, fractions, decimals, and integers.
- The ability to make and use measurements in both traditional and metric units.
- The ability to use effectively the mathematics of:
  —Integers, fractions, and decimals.
  —Ratios, proportions, and percentages.
  —Roots and powers.
  —Algebra.
  —Geometry.
- The ability to make estimates and approximations, and to judge the reasonableness of a result.
- The ability to formulate and solve a problem in mathematical terms.
- The ability to select and use approximate approaches and tools in solving problems (mental computation, trial and error, paper-and-pencil techniques, calculator, and computer).
- The ability to use elementary concepts of probability and statistics.

Reasoning

- The ability to identify and formulate problems, as well as the ability to propose and evaluate ways to solve them.
- The ability to recognize and use inductive and deductive reasoning, and to recognize fallacies in reasoning.
- The ability to draw reasonable conclusions from information found in various sources, whether written, spoken, or displayed in tables and graphs, and to defend one's conclusions rationally.

- The ability to comprehend, develop, and use concepts and generalizations.
- The ability to distinguish between fact and opinion.

Studying

This set of abilities is different in kind from those that precede it. They are set forth here because they constitute the key abilities in learning how to learn. Successful study skills are necessary for acquiring the other five competencies as well as for achieving the desired outcomes in the Basic Academic Subjects. Students are unlikely to be efficient in any part of their work without these study skills.

- The ability to set study goals and priorities consistent with stated course objectives and one's own progress, to establish surroundings and habits conducive to learning independently or with others, and to follow a schedule that accounts for both short- and long-term projects.
- The ability to locate and use resources external to the classroom (for example, libraries, computers, interviews, and direct observation), and to incorporate knowledge from such sources into the learning process.
- The ability to develop and use general and specialized vocabularies, and to use them for reading, writing, speaking, listening, computing, and studying.
- The ability to understand and to follow customary instructions for academic work in order to recall, comprehend, analyze, summarize, and report the main ideas from reading, lectures, and other academic experiences; and to synthesize knowledge and apply it to new situations.
- The ability to prepare for various types of examinations and to devise strategies for pacing, attempting or omitting questions, thinking, writing, and editing according to the type of examination; to satisfy other assessments of learning in meeting course objectives such as laboratory performance, class participation, simulation, and students' evaluations.
- The ability to accept constructive criticism and learn from it.

Cawelti, Boyer, and Broudy models (Figure 7) as a guide so that they could create their own model, which included seven basic areas: (1) basic skills; (2) manipulation of symbols; (3) man's relationship to man; (4) man's understanding of his environment; (5) man's understanding of the past; (6) physical and mental fitness; and (7) basic survival skills. The Ames model (Figure 8) was a blend and adaptation of Boyer's Common Learnings and the College Board materials.

Four schools developed their own models. San Rafael worked from a "zero-based" curriculum development model. First, the committee

Figure 7. Models of General Education

Broudy	Cawelti	Boyer
Basic Sciences	Science-Technology	Relationship with Nature
Aesthetic Studies Exemplary	Cultural Studies	Values and Beliefs
Molar (Social) Problems	Citizenship-Societal Studies	Membership in Groups and Institutions
Symbolic Studies	Health-Recreation-Leisure	Use of Symbols
Developmental Studies	Learning-Communicating Thinking Skills	Sense of Time
		Producing and Consuming

considered what educational experiences were of most worth. Next, the committee studied the goal statement of a fellow school district. They then constructed an outline of "Commonalities in Learning—Skills and Understanding," and cross-referenced this outline to San Rafael's extant high school courses. Included in the outline were: (1) communication skills—written, oral, and aural; (2) computation; (3) understanding of and skills in technology; (4) understanding of the human machine; (5) understanding of man's relationship with nature; (6) understanding of values and value judgments: cultural differences; (7) interpersonal relationships: the world view; (8) understanding of the arts: and extension of communications; (9) research skills; (10) survival skills; and (11) leisure skills. In retrospect, some teachers in San Rafael felt that the zero-based approach was a great starting point, but that it didn't serve their long-term purposes. They felt it required too much work.

Ventura and Buena High Schools shared the same model. At first they worked separately, then together, to draw up a consensus framework organized around six curriculum areas (Figure 9). In addition to these six areas, the school's goals are broken down under four branches of learning and several subgoals. Each branch of learning demands an activity: (1) Specific Information (The Body of Knowledge): Know That . . . ; (2) Basic Skills: Know How . . . ; (3) Process

Figure 8. The Ames Model

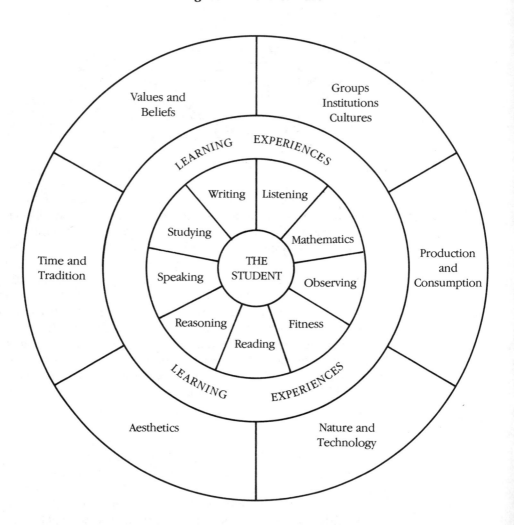

Figure 9. The Ventura Model

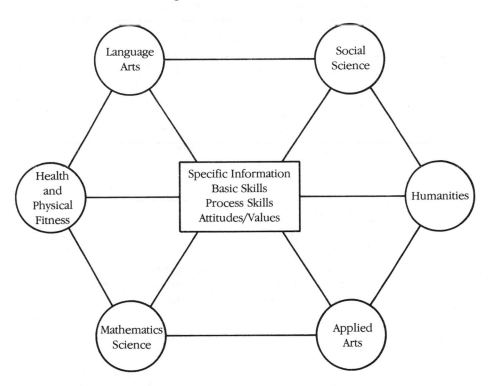

Skills: Understand Implications ...; and (4) Attitudes and Values: Appreciate ....

Ventura Principal Bob Cousar felt strongly about using such a model. "Any task force has to use their model as an instrument. They have to ask, 'Is there a fit between what you say you want to do and what you are doing?' If what we are doing doesn't fit our design, then why are we doing it?"

In Baltimore both the Woodlawn High School Dimensions Study Group and the Baltimore County Study Group came up with definitions that were patterned with almost the same goals in mind. From these definitions Baltimore County wrote its own model that reflected the logo, "The Educated Person" (Figure 10).

Carlsbad was the only school that neither used nor developed a model. They found it impossible to think about what general education ought to be when they were "working in a real world with real constraints." When the New Mexico State Department of Education mandated changes in educational standards for its schools, Carlsbad felt that the changes impeded their curriculum study progress. As we will see, activities at the state level would eventually have their impact on other network schools.

Outcome Statements

After selecting a model for their projects, most schools drafted an outcome statement that would articulate the more specific goals and objectives that they hoped would come out of the model. In general, their priorities concerned competencies and learning as well as an overall regard for the student, or as Scarsdale put it,

> What students should be able to do, and what they should know that would enable them to continue learning in the future, to be productive members of society, and to enjoy life more fully.

Four schools referred to these statements as "goals"; three called them "common learnings"; two termed them "educational or common teaching objectives"; and the others used titles such as "general principles," "learning experiences," or "elements."

The names are not important. What *is* important is the tremendous amount of work that schools put into these learning outcome statements and what they eventually did with these statements. In a few

Figure 10. Baltimore County Senior High School Program Goals

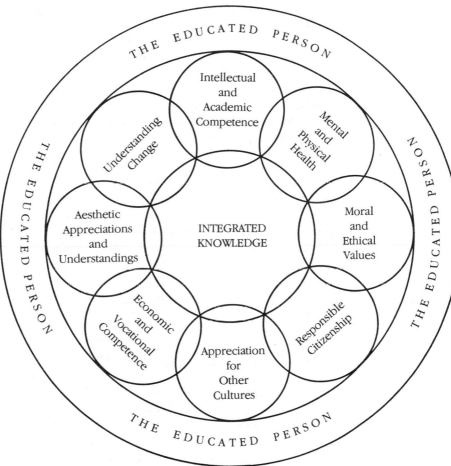

schools the process of putting together these lists has not been completed.

Carlsbad, for example, ideally hopes to identify concepts and process skills and establish a sequence of skill acquisition. The achievement of any overall goals must be tackled, they feel, by all K-12
personnel. So far this has not worked out, according to committee

members. Attempts have been made, but people are seen as being "attuned to courses, so changes in course offerings have been tackled first. By starting at the course level the committee hopes that they can work back to concepts." As a step in this direction, during the 1983-1984 school year, teachers are looking at the objectives for, and activities in, every class being taught in the school.

Ann Arbor, as we have pointed out, is also still in process. Before the process was redefined and rescheduled, the two committees working together with the administration suggested "those common learnings that all students are expected to acquire through their participation in a required instructional program." These are the common learnings that "constitute an outline of a proposed general education program for all Ann Arbor high school students in grades 9 through 12." These common learnings are now under discussion. Originally, to give some sense of what took place, there were ten "cross-disciplinary" categories, each of which included from three to 19 specific learnings: citizenship, career development, reading, writing, speaking and listening, reasoning, mathematics, computer competency, library skills, study skills. In addition, the following disciplinary categories contained from nine to 32 specific learnings: English language and literature, health and physical education, mathematics, social studies, and visual performing arts. However, at publication time these categories and specific learnings are still *proposed,* and as such are subject to change.

To date, approximately half of the schools—Page, Denver, San Rafael, Ames, Oak Park, Largo, and the two Ventura schools—have based their subsequent efforts on a thorough definition and articulation of the outcomes first, followed by a realignment of the experiences or courses that best fit these outcomes. The other districts in one way or another have stressed courses and/or graduation requirements to a much greater extent than they have addressed specific outcomes.

The schools that stressed courses and graduation requirements have reported that they now need to go back and think through what will be taught in the courses, especially any courses that are additions to graduation requirements.

At first reading, this difference may seem a lot like "which came first, the chicken or the egg?" In the seven schools that did thoroughly define the outcomes/learnings first, we heard comments such as:

> Some network schools talked a good game, but the changes they made were mostly cosmetic, or else they changed graduation requirements but didn't really get at the common learnings.

> Unlike some of the others [schools], we didn't just look at course titles or graduation requirements. We remained truer to the original concept than most.

> We wanted to find the holes and we did.

> We wanted to look at the experiences kids should have rather than courses.

> We were looking at the important cross-disciplinary concepts that students should have; we didn't care in what subjects they would be taught.

Such comments may have arisen from competitiveness; nevertheless, more often than not, teachers in these schools sincerely believed that they had been truer to the concept of the ASCD project in proceeding along this path: "It's harder and more time consuming, but we know that we have a more solid foundation on which to make *any* future decisions." At the beginning of the project all of the schools followed roughly similar steps; however, the decision about *outcomes versus courses/graduation requirements* stands out as a true fork in the road. Moreover, even for those schools that decided to build from the outcomes up, the means they used varied, as did the sophistication of these means.

Buena and Ventura, as mentioned earlier, adopted a model that centered on six curriculum areas and four branches of learning (see Figure 9). Under each curriculum area, the branches of learning are broken down into several subgoals. Once the model building process was completed, the two principals met with their department chairpersons to determine exactly where in the then-required courses each student was encountering the identified areas and goals of study. If the requisite course work was found lacking, the departments were asked to determine when and how the goals should be included in order to implement the plan.

Denver's East High drew up five pages of "General Principles." Steering committee members saw these principles as heavily weighted in the areas of mathematics and English: "We're trying to get people to make a conscious effort to teach math and English in every area." "It's a general list, which I wish was more specific," said one key leader, "but we've made a commitment to what we think is important." Another teacher felt strongly that the commitment to mathematics should be expressed in terms of survival skills.

In Page, a survey was developed that listed concepts and skills that the steering committee thought should be taught. To arrive at a consensus of educational objectives, the survey was submitted to the faculty on two occasions for their suggestions. During the summer of 1982, three members of the general education committee developed a mapping system wherein each skill or concept was compared to the goals and objectives of Page High School's existing curriculum. They discovered that several objectives were already being taught to 100 percent of the student body. To get a better understanding of the weak areas, the committee tested the 1982-83 graduating seniors. Tests were written by faculty members in the identified areas of weakness: consumer math skills, food and nutrition, survival skills, general automotive skills, and art and music appreciation. In some cases a few faculty members also took these tests so that their general education in these areas could be compared with the students. During the summer of 1983 all data were collected and analyzed, and a set of recommendations compiled.

Both San Rafael and Pinellas Park involved their faculties in designing a comprehensive list of objectives. In Pinellas Park, the faculty originally listed 145 cross-disciplinary concepts, which—unlike some of the other schools—were not derived from the College Board's *Academic Preparation for College.* After a second examination of this list, the number of concepts was pared down to 105 concepts (Appendix A). As in Page, the Pinellas Park leadership used an instrument to see how well these concepts were being presented in the school's classes. Basically, teachers were asked to rate on a five-point scale to what degree they were covering the 105 common learnings. A cross-departmental committee, which included members of the steering committee, studied the responses. Assistant Principal Dorothy Cheatham admitted that this instrument was not "scientific"; nevertheless, she felt that the cross-departmental committee guarded against teachers who would overestimate what they were actually covering in their classes. The goal was to find out what was being covered and to what extent, not how well the learnings were being mastered. The final stage was to do something with these results.

Ames's Sub-Cardinal Principles

The steering committee and the faculty in Ames also developed an inventory instrument. A total of 89 objectives was identified, including 41 skills adopted from the College Board's competencies and 48 knowledge elements in six categories that reflect Boyer's six commonalities (for the latter, see Appendix B). This instrument included the skills and knowledge elements that the Ames faculty felt all students should experience before graduation. The steering committee then developed an instrument so that an inventory of the present curriculum could be done to see how it fit the definition of general education and the 89 elements. Constructing this instrument took time, as did the workshops to orient the faculty to the instrument.

After the first inventory was completed, the steering committee reviewed the results. They felt that some teachers in some subjects had claimed too much: "Since the _____ department claimed to be doing practically every one of the 89 elements, we could have kept the _____ department and eliminated all the others." No one found this very surprising. "Some people were worried about keeping their classes alive so they won't be RIFed." After refining the inventory technique, they decided to do a second inventory.

An analysis of a sample of 100 student transcripts from the class of 1982 revealed that a high percentage of students *were* being exposed to the objectives in the general education model. However, Ames High School Principal Ralph Farrar and Superintendent of Schools Paul Masem realized that the first two inventories had effectively determined neither the quality of what was being taught nor the degree to which it was being taught. Hence, the third inventory was designed. This time teachers were asked not only to describe the elements included in each of the courses but also to give: (1) typical operational objectives based on the element, (2) typical teaching strategies that were used, and (3) typical methods for monitoring student progress based on the objective. Teachers were asked to do this for each different preparation they taught and to be "tougher" in the future in the way they reviewed each element. Final results, "What the Data

Reveal," were reported to the faculty.

Teachers liked this impressive effort because it focused on the classroom. As one teacher told us, the effort led him to four "obvious" conclusions:

1. Discussion and sharing is needed at the department level.

2. More emphasis must be placed on the art of teaching—we can't know enough about how to do too many things.

3. The administration is really trying to help us with fine tuning.

4. Nothing will get done unless we are a community.

The hardest part was staying on-task: "We wouldn't have gotten as far as we did without the committee to bring us back into focus." Part of the problem, according to one teacher, was that the 89 points, or the points on any list, are abstract and people aren't sure what they mean:

> Every concept has a territory of meaning. If people can't agree on that "territory," or if they drift away from their decision, then the redefinition process is headed for trouble.

Superintendent Masem saw the Ames list of 89 elements as being "Sub-Cardinal Principles," a reference to the 1918 document *The Seven Cardinal Principles* [5] published by the NEA Commission on the Reorganization of Secondary Education. Masem felt that the training teachers get in schools of education has caused them to internalize elements such as those on the list of 89, "This is 'the party line,' and it shows up in our list of universals."

Many teachers may think this way, but not all. We talked with physics teachers in two different school systems who questioned whether or not there is anything in physics that everyone needs to know. One teacher was cynical about being asked to come up with a list whether or not he agreed with the ideal of common learnings. "If common learnings are going to become the curriculum, then we will come up with a list to protect ourselves, but I don't feel good about what we did." These teachers felt strongly that everyone needs science but not necessarily physics. The major fear was that everyone might be required to take a watered-down physics course that wasn't really physics at all. Other science teachers vehemently disagreed with this position but agreed that it made them think about the issues of what was universal and how to face the issue of universality versus quality.

Universality vs. Quality

Oak Park addressed this issue head on in their Proposal for General Education. They felt that a teacher might balk at the word *must* as in "must have" or "must experience." Anyone or any group who chooses what is of most worth may well be guilty of arrogance in choosing for others.

> Is it possible to make a list of learning experiences to be required of all students without being arbitrary and without operating from raw personal preference? In response to this question, the philosopher-teacher will offer a qualified "yes, if." If the list of such experiences has been developed using a principle of selection that recognizes the nature of the world in which students will be living and working, its *must's* should not be alarming. If the list of such experiences is based on responsible predictions about the 21st century, the time in which today's students will spend the most productive part of their lives, it will be redeemed from raw personal preference.

To get a broad view of what their experiences might be, the Oak Park Committee used the first semester of 1982-83 to sample 251 persons from among the faculty, administration, a Citizens Council, Parents Human Relations Committee, and Student Council. Participants were asked to sort the learning experiences (see Appendix C) that had been collected by the committee and the school's department chairs into three categories:

Category A—those learning experiences that should definitely be included in a general education program and should be required of all students.

Category B—those learning experiences that should definitely be included in a general education program, but for which some agency other than the school should have primary responsibility.

Category C—those learning experiences that should not be part of a general education program.

The set of learning experiences labeled "skills for lifelong learning" drew a heavy Category A response as did "fostering a sense of global consciousness," with the exception of item 13, "developing an appreciation of universal values such as honesty, justice, and kindness," which fell somewhat more heavily in the Category B. Written comments questioned item 13 because of its assumption that such universal values exist. In many cases neither students nor their parents wanted the school primarily involved in teaching values. Teaching values was seen as a prime responsibility of the home. Learning experiences that would "engender a sense of self-worth" all drew heavier Category A than B or C responses, but not by as nearly as wide a margin as did the other two major sections.

Based on these results and the additional written comments, the committee decided to consider the value statements to be subjects of philosophical inquiry rather than assumed values to be appreciated. Item 13 was dropped, and the words *philosophical* and *scientific* were added to items 8 and 9. Other schools (for instance, Baltimore) took a much stronger stance on the inclusion of values study in the curriculum; but as Oak Park Associate Principal Donald Offerman reminded us, the process and the results grow out of the ethos of each community.

The amended list was submitted to the Oak Park department heads as a "statement of the ideal curriculum against which the existing curriculum should be measured." All department heads then held discussions with the faculty members in their departments. The responses were recorded on an instrument to measure the extent to which:

1. A desired learning experience was represented in the courses required of all students.

2. That experience was represented in the first elective typically selected in departments without required courses.

3. That experience was represented in the total collection of courses available in the school.

Department heads rated the extent of coverage using a four-point Likert Scale. When the results were graphed, the school could see its strengths and weaknesses. The teachers concluded that some elements missing in the required program could be found elsewhere in the curriculum, although in a few cases the elements were weak in all segments of the program.

Oak Park didn't have much difficulty in obtaining information about how its existing curriculum measured up against the ideal. There didn't seem to be much defensiveness or protection of a department's turf. In fact, respondents seemed surprised that anyone would ask about defensiveness or turf:

> Don Offerman asked us to evaluate for deficiencies, and we tried to be honest. I guess it was too early in our deliberations to see what might happen. Our enrollments are stable, and we like this process that we're going through.

This sense of security and community in Oak Park is much stronger than in most U.S. schools today and may account for the greater degree of openness. This finding agrees with Sara Lawrence Lightfoot's observation of good high schools. [6]

Putting the Graduation Requirements Before the Course Content

In considering the schools that emphasized courses and/or graduation requirements first, then backtracked to reexamine specifically what would be done in these courses, we were not surprised to discover that two of the three are in large districts—New Orleans and Baltimore County. Both schools, O. Perry Walker and Woodlawn, must coordinate their efforts with those of a much larger group of schools and a systemwide curriculum, which makes redefinition and change excruciatingly complex. Making changes based on the traditional Carnegie unit course seems to be the best route. Pinellas Park and East High, both of which began with learning outcomes, have also had to cope with this complexity. In the spring of 1984, County Assistant Superintendent of Secondary Education Kenneth Webster was still in the process of taking the Pinellas Park common learnings to the other county schools. The possible impact of the work done at East High on the rest of the Denver system wasn't clear at the time of our interviews. Was a course-first approach, therefore, a quicker way to bring about change?

The evidence does not suggest that it is. Either approach seems to take a long time. Baltimore County and New Orleans are prime examples. As mentioned earlier, Woodlawn High School's Dimensions study was part of a much larger Baltimore County project. The Dimensions study reflects a set of goals and objectives as well as an enormous effort expended to develop a hierarchy of concepts in the various subject matter areas. For example, in an art course every youngster will study certain concepts, but at the level most appropriate to that youngster, whether at the most basic level, a standard level, or in the range of the gifted and talented. All art teachers will have a curriculum guide for all grades K-12, so that they can see the concepts taught at each grade level. Each guide will illustrate how each concept might be taught in a measurable way. These examples are only starting points, but they are included in the curriculum guides to make these documents as useful as possible. However, in spite of all the work done thus far to create these concepts and guides, as well as to make other changes that we will explore later, Baltimore administrators realize that there is still more to be done. In particular, Assistant Superintendent Ben Ebersole hopes to make connections and correlations between subjects (for instance, between science and social studies) to try to make the final curriculum far more interdisciplinary. A report will also be issued shortly on the teaching of values, since Baltimore County has decided to teach ethics.

Baltimore County has a considerable head start over the other large systems, in part because they had already begun their examination of the high school curriculum long before the network began, and also because Woodlawn High School had been involved in the entire county undertaking. The same is not true for O. Perry Walker High School in New Orleans. At O. Perry Walker each department was asked to examine the content of its courses and to rethink the goals and objectives of these courses. To date, about 90 goals for the individual subject disciplines have been created, and a model curriculum has been written. In rethinking the courses, the faculty has also begun to emphasize learning outcomes. They still need to decide on content for the model curriculum, and as yet are not ready to make a proposal for change to the superintendent and board of education. It is still unclear what impact the ASCD project will have on other high schools in New Orleans. As was true for the other large districts, regardless of whether they emphasized learning outcomes or courses first, the process takes a long time. But sooner or later decisions about learning outcomes will result.

This also seems to hold true for Scarsdale. The Scarsdale committee spent its time debating the courses that students must study. Keeping in mind the rapid advances in science and technology and the effect of these advances on our daily lives, they soon realized that students' experiences involve much more than mere technology: students live lives of feeling and expression as well. The committee felt that "the school must encourage students in understanding themselves and others through creative experiences that actively involve students in the emotional life that art provides."

These deliberations have led to changes in graduation require-ments and a reexamination of what is included in these courses, as well as the sequence in which the courses are taught. The English department has agreed on general concepts; for example, all 9th graders may read certain books, but they may also read poetry with the choice of specific poems left up to the teacher, who will select what is most appropriate for a given group of students. Thus, there are commonalities as well as a range of choices.

Principal Ronald Barnes hopes that the effort in Scarsdale will eventually lead to more cross-departmental teaching. He supports the effort to list skills, as do teachers and administrators in all of the schools; further, he envisions the list of skills (or learning outcomes) as much more than just a neatly typed document that no one pays attention to. Many schools that have established learning outcomes have not yet found this to be a problem. People are still paying attention; however, if the process that initially developed the out-comes is not kept alive, the problem could arise. But we agreed that the cross-disciplinary dialogue that led to the learning outcomes in the ASCD network helped to decrease a sense of faculty isolation in many schools. Many teachers and administrators believe strongly that if this dialogue is not kept alive, isolation may reappear.

We believe that the degree of ownership and involvement is higher in those schools that have built from the learning outcomes/common learnings to course and graduation requirement changes. Although the technique is not faster than going straight from a model to gradua-tion requirements and course changes, in the long run it seems more effective. When people see *their* model and *their* learning outcomes, they feel a powerful sense of individual and shared ownership. This sense of ownership is the *sine qua non* of true curriculum change. Without it there can be no genuine improvement behind the closed classroom door.

Territoriality

As the schools moved to create outcome statements, courses, and new graduation requirements, teachers inevitably began to worry about their turf. Were some departments going to be "winners" and others "losers" as a result of the redefinition process? Privately, teachers asked, "Why do other departments have more to teach while ours has less?" "Am I going to lose my job because of cutbacks in the number of electives that are offered?" "Do I dare let this happen?"

Most of the network schools have undergone the same pressures that *all* American high schools have endured within the past decade: declining enrollments, closings, consolidations, and RIFs. Some teachers, especially at the beginning of the process, worried that network activities might cause insecure faculty members even more anxiety. Some teachers suspected that certain administrators had a hidden agenda. Some even questioned other teachers' motives for volunteering to be in the network in the first place. These concerns did not emerge in some schools until teachers began to realize how things were going to turn out; for instance, which subjects would be taught more and which would be taught less.

In Oak Park, for example, teachers had concerns about who would teach computer use and who would do the additional work in speech. In this instance, the question was satisfactorily answered by deciding that these were common learnings that all teachers would teach in virtually every subject. The same was true in using computers. To date, more than 100 teachers have had inservice training; and additional work with computers is either being planned or is already in operation in every area of the curriculum except physical education and driver education.

Not all schools have resolved the problems quite so neatly. Some vocational teachers were worried that the emphasis on general education would hurt their programs. This feeling was more prevalent in the early stages of the process. As time progressed, many vocational teachers believed that they would always get their share of students:

> After all, we teach many general education principles as well—pride in work, promptness, neatness, and giving an honest day's work for an honest day's wage. These are things that every youngster should know.

A vocational teacher in Page worried about balance between vocational and general education:

> How much math and science is "enough," especially in a town like Page where only 20 percent of the kids are going on to college? What's best for that 20 percent?

Other vocational education teachers—as did several elective teachers—firmly believed that not enough was being done in certain core subject areas. Even though it might endanger their jobs, they wanted to see students learn more in math or science, or whatever the area might be.

As the projects progressed, some teachers might well have become concerned by the proposed changes. As one teacher in New Orleans put it, "The elective teachers came unglued when they realized what might happen." In fact, in most schools we visited, the number of electives was being cut back dramatically. For example, driver education faced a precarious future as a part of the daily curriculum.

Physical education teachers faced significant cuts in some schools, although Barbara Hall, a Buena High School physical education teacher, wondered if we aren't sending our American public mixed signals:

> Where are students going to get the physical skills? We are constantly told that our society is moving to a shorter work week. Where are students going to learn about recreational activities? Can't people see that there's a core program in physical education, too—common learnings that all students should have?

A thoughtful physical education teacher in Carlsbad voiced a different viewpoint:

> I'm prejudiced against terminal ignorance. Physical education, especially at the elementary level, is nothing but glorified recess. We've got a good program here. It's not "run-em-till-they-puke" as in so many schools. But not enough programs are as well organized as ours.

Her real concern, once again, is that in physical education, as in all areas, teachers have to look at the concepts they are teaching, "More is not necessarily better, in physical education or in any other subject."

We heard similar comments from other teachers in other areas. Many were insightful; a few were defensive. Our biggest surprise was that we heard relatively few comments about turf and territoriality.

Perhaps by the time of our school visits (fall 1983) many, if not most, of the issues had been worked out. Schools such as Pinellas Park and Scarsdale reported that there never had been much concern about territoriality. San Rafael downplayed the fact that the school was part of an ASCD network:

> We were concerned with *our* needs. We didn't dwell on ASCD. This seemed to create less pressure.

The schools that had defined a set of learning outcomes to be taught throughout the curriculum seemed to suffer the fewest problems, by far; however, other schools had largely worked out their problems, too. Indeed, we saw some examples of "fenced-in turf" teachers who were uncertain that they wanted to teach a new and previously unknown group of students. For example, in a few schools, particularly in art and advanced mathematics and science courses, where certain teachers were accustomed to working with able and talented students, broadening or adding to the curriculum meant that they would ultimately have to work with students who might be neither talented nor motivated. Some teachers were not sure that they really wanted to do this. They felt that they would have to "water down" the curriculum, and the result would be that their better students would suffer.

In spite of these exceptions, it was a pleasant surprise to see how relatively moderate the turf issues actually were. We are told how difficult it is to get people to change, and that indeed had been a problem; however, true blocking behavior was rare. The most insidious problem from the beginning, according to several steering committee members, was passivity: "Too many teachers simply didn't want to get involved."

4 The Students

In visiting the network schools, we looked forward to talking to a wide range of students. We wanted the chance to ask high school students how they felt about changes in schooling that are going to affect their lives. Since we were to visit a diverse and far-flung group of high schools, we were also curious to see how these young people were alike and how they were different in their attitudes toward school.

Although I had taught high school social studies for ten years, since that time most of my work as a college professor of curriculum development has meant working with teachers. I had not had the opportunity to work closely with high school students in recent years except in one high school, which was part of a Teacher Corps Project that I directed from 1978-1982.

How had teenagers changed since my days as a teacher? Are the reports that we read in *Time, Newsweek, Phi Delta Kappan,* and *Educational Leadership* accurate, or are we reading glittering generalities and stereotypes that make teenagers easier to pigeonhole and, thus, deal with? Vietnam is history; issues of race and gender are not as actively and vocally advanced as they were only a few short years ago. These times are quieter. What does all this mean as far as young people are concerned?

Talking With Students

To get some highly unscientific answers to these questions in each network school, we asked for a chance to talk informally with representatives of the student body. "Don't set up anything formal. Just give us a chance to talk to students who are free at the same times we are."

We specifically asked, "Don't give us just the kids who are 'A' students, write for *Harper's,* or have begun their Nobel prize acceptance speeches. Let us talk to a variety of students." The schools really tried; but in most cases if we didn't get the very best and the brightest, we were only a rung lower. If nothing else, we came away assured that these high schools have many bright and capable young men and women.

Pioneer High School gave us a chance to talk to students at random. We were taken to a small afternoon study hall and told, "Help yourselves." A couple of students politely refused to talk to us—they would have a math test tomorrow. (As one writer so aptly put it, "Don't worry about constitutional amendments. As long as there are math tests, there will be school prayer.") Others were willing to talk (we imagined them wondering what we were selling—class rings, colleges, term insurance?). Their answers were hesitant at first and not very articulate. At best these were "C" students, according to the students themselves. Most doubted if they would go on to college, maybe junior college but even that was doubtful. The most important thing right now was to make it through high school. But yes, they liked their school. Their teachers were OK (a mighty accolade). Why? Because they cared. They treated students as individuals. They knew their names. They were willing to help. The students had heard that they were going to have to take more math and science. They knew that a lot of adults were unhappy with high schools. The homework load was becoming a lot heavier, but the teachers must know what was best for them. However, they hoped that they'd still be able to take some courses that would help them get jobs after finishing school. They hoped that requirements wouldn't get so tough that they couldn't graduate. In any event, they'd keep on trying.

Students' Concerns

So very serious! And yet these thoughts echoed comments that we heard over and over in many schools. Students liked their teachers. They liked school, and school was no joke. As a student leader in Carlsbad told us, "School is the outpost of civilization." Another added, "There's too much negativism about education, but we do want the best we can get." Asked what that best might be, the reply in Carlsbad was "more advanced courses in economics, government, business, and accounting, in addition to the usual math and science."

The economics theme kept coming up in most schools. The students wanted to take courses that would either help them get jobs after school or get them into college. Teachers felt that students were far more compliant and willing to meet conventions in a time of economic uncertainty. Student leaders worried about the loss of vocational education programs for non-college-bound students. In Pinellas Park, students on the principal's advisory committee wanted more emphasis on writing term papers so that they would be ready for college. They wanted to start studying foreign languages earlier. Several argued for fewer electives, noting parenthetically that everyone should do some work in the arts and humanities. These sentiments were largely seconded by students in Ames, Iowa.

But some students vigorously disagreed. They were tired of taking the same old thing, especially just to raise their grade point averages. They worried that "this school is more concerned with discipline than our education. We need to try something different, for example, a course in computer literacy." Other students felt there was enough variety in course selection. Still others gave their teachers a vote of confidence. "They spend a lot of time with kids. They know our names. Some show up for games and other events. That's important." In Ames, a cross section of students appreciated the fact that teachers gave them the chance to be creative. The expectations were high, but there was a wide variety of classes and levels in subjects such as chemistry. Teachers had an assigned free period during which they were available for students who needed that help.

At Buena High School, a group of bright students observed that a good teacher should have up-to-date knowledge of his or her subject matter and enthusiasm for teaching that subject matter. They wanted their teachers to help them with their mistakes so that they wouldn't repeat them, and they also wanted freedom to do or not do homework depending on how well they knew what they were doing.

In every school we visited, there was a strong sense of school pride. School trophy cases were bulging with awards, most of them athletic, although many students pointed with pride to service and scholarly awards as well. Students at O. Perry Walker, which boasts 35 school organizations in addition to its sports teams, were proud that their school had won the Mayor's Award for Community Involvement three of the last four years. Students in other schools echoed another recurrent theme, "Maybe we're not the best, but its important to think that you're good. If you think you're number one, you'll try harder."

Obviously, not all students share these opinions. As suggested, our visitor's deck was stacked with more student body leaders and good students than it was with potential dropouts and troublemakers. Every school has its own social structure, and in this social structure there are cliques with different names depending on the location— Preppies, Brainiacs, Dirt Heads (a variant on yesterday's Greaser), Bleacher Creatures (the place to hang out and smoke in one school), and Burnouts, who are often bright students who do their work in class but, as other students described them, "have a tough guy image, smoke, and are rude." These are just a few of the groups. How students feel about school depends on where they fit into the social structure.

When we—perhaps naively—asked about drugs and alcohol, students answered sincerely: they're there. Anyone can get drugs in any of the high schools we visited, and some do; but apparently the choice for most students, if they decide to choose at all, is alcohol. Although many students said that they didn't feel any pressure to use either drugs or alcohol, many principals are not sure they agree with these statements. Pioneer High School Principal Milo White in Ann Arbor thought drug and alcohol use in high schools was well-camouflaged. He thought that schools have to come up with alternative highs; that is, intellectual highs. Adolescents need a warm, supportive environment. Athletics and school activities may help, but we also need community intervention programs as well, such as nonalcoholic proms and parties.

Looking Toward the Future

The best and brightest kids realize that they live in a world where they are expected to meet the high expectations of their parents and the schools. We asked a group of 9th graders in Scarsdale what they wanted to do with their lives. One vivacious young student told us breathlessly of her desire to be a dancer. I asked how her parents felt about this "No problem," she bubbled. "My Dad says once I finish medical school, I can do anything I want."

One of the expectations that the brighter students do *not* have is to teach. Of more than 100 students that we talked to, only four expressed a desire to become a teacher. Why not? "Too much hard work. Teachers don't get paid much. And who'd want to work with kids like me?"

By far the most frequent career choice we heard was "accountant." Students may agree that their communities are far too materialistic, yet in the next sentence they told us their dreams: a nice home, a car, and all other accoutrements of the good life that their parents have or wish they had.

They also liked living where they do. While a few college-bound students had no desire to return, most students liked where they had grown up and intended to stay or return once they had finished their education. Indeed, in most of the schools a significant percentage of the faculty had gone through the school system themselves. This percentage often came as a total surprise to the current leadership, a finding that raises some interesting questions about teacher mobility. As some teachers also told us, "You'd be surprised at how many of those students who say they don't want to live here will eventually return."

Another phenomenon we discovered is how parents, especially black parents, in heavily populated areas, will fight to get their children into some of the network schools considered outstanding. For the affluent it is relatively easy to move into an Ann Arbor, San Rafael, or Scarsdale, to name only three. It is not so easy for those who are poor. However, in school systems such as Baltimore County and Oak Park, two systems that volunteered the information, a significant number of "illegal" students live with relatives or friends or somehow establish a postal address in order to attend a school perceived as one that will give them a head start in life.

O. Perry Walker has maintained much of its enrollments because a large number of black students prefer to attend the school over other high schools in New Orleans. It is seen as "the place to go if you want to go on to college." Unfortunately, it is often too late for many of these youngsters. Many do not do well for a number of reasons, the most important one of which, school officials feel, is that these students have a weaker academic foundation than those who have come through an entire system, K-12. Students who had had that base, whatever their race, sex, or ethnic background, were far more likely to succeed.

The Role of the School

The significance of the school among teenagers varies considerably throughout the country. In rural areas such as Carlsbad or Page, the school is not only the focus of student life; it also plays a major role in the community. In Carlsbad, students and faculty worried about restricting electives for more required courses. If electives were restricted, the school band and color guard might be lost. In Ames, the students liked the idea of an eight-period day. They feared that a school day with fewer periods might eliminate the band and school newspaper, which were now part of the school day. These activities were important parts of the school program; they made the academics more tolerable even for the brightest students.

In California the story was different. Repeatedly, in Ventura and in San Rafael we heard students, teachers, administrators, and parents say that the school simply wasn't the center of life the way it was in many other parts of the country. There were too many distractions: beaches, mountains, jobs, San Francisco, Los Angeles, and so on. On a warm, beautiful day a school may show an 18 percent absentee rate as a result of beach attendance.

Several adults agreed that too many California youngsters have their priorities confused or else don't know better. As one Buena High School teacher originally from the Midwest put it, "When we were young, we knew school was our number one priority, even if we didn't follow through on that knowledge. Now it may be a car, a job, whatever." Many teachers argued that their students work for luxuries rather than necessities. Another teacher added, "There are too many dances, too much fun and games, and so on. We have far too few merit finalists or semi-finalists for a school this size." We hasten to point out that we heard the same comment, not only in the Golden State, but in other schools around the country.

The Search for a Balanced Curriculum

The ASCD process was an important vehicle to reexamine what the schools are doing, especially to see if there's too much fragmentation of learning. In California, many people wanted to raise expectations for students. But the question remains: What is the proper balance? How much is enough? In several of the network schools the pendulum may be swinging so far to a mandated core curriculum that students may have little room to explore, to see what they may want to do with their lives, both vocationally and avocationally. Many college-bound students told us that they have little choice. It appears that this condition will get worse. As one representative senior told us, "I'd like to take a course in computers. I know it's important, but I can't fit it into my program." Others were glad they were not 9th graders, "Right now there are *three different sets* of graduation requirements for grades 9-12."

Answers to our questions about homework varied from school to school. "I don't know who collects all that data about kids watching television," one active junior commented, "but my friends and I sure aren't watching it." Others were willing to admit that they should be doing more homework but don't. Unlike in the past, few students in the network high schools had the chance to do homework in a study hall. In a few cases, study halls were mandated for 9th graders but after that are a rarity. A year ago, the study halls in Baltimore County's Woodlawn High School were filled to capacity. Not so today. Most educators and parents would agree that this is a more efficient use of the school day; however, how much work should be assigned *after* the school day is over?

One comment we heard repeatedly from students was that the only time they read for pleasure or read anything outside of school was during the summer. "There's just not enough time during the school year." I've heard my own children say this. And yet I think of my own childhood and that of my wife and the joy we took in reading. The majority of my friends made the same comment. How many of us were told by our parents that our eyes would go bad if we didn't stop reading all the time? How many of us were caught under the blankets reading by flashlight? Has the pendulum swung too far to the opposite side? In Page, Flo Wynn of the Reading Department had begun a family reading program, which had enrolled over 100 families of high school students; but her program appeared to be an exception. A few network high school libraries are well used, but more often than not students (and teachers) said that they didn't go to the library unless they needed to look up something.

Teachers and administrators in every district argued that all students, "even the bright kids," need to be more well-rounded. Everyone needs help with the skills for living and getting along with others. East High in Denver has a Shakespeare course that integrates not only the races but also "street-wise and scholarly kids." A mathematics teacher feels that this well-taught course helps both groups of students, since each brings a fresh perspective to what is being taught.

We asked people how they felt about the relationship between tracking and a general or core education. Some teachers felt strongly that there was too much tracking; still others would have it no other way. But most are resigned to its inevitability. "The schedule is always going to track students to some extent." It was not a burning issue to most of the people we interviewed.

While a few teachers missed the good old days of the late 1960s and early 1970s (they enjoyed the challenge and excitement of the period), most did not. "The 60s were downright dangerous, but we got through them. The kids are a lot more passive now."

We agree that much of their learning is passive. In far too many of the classes we visited, teachers lectured, while students listened and took notes. So what else is new? Isn't that the way it has always been? My wife Christine, a departmental colleague and constant companion on these visits, shed a new light on classroom visits. A former elementary teacher with virtually no training or experience at the high school level, Christine teaches elementary curriculum and methods and supervises elementary student teachers. To put it mildly, Christine was uneasy in her observations. Accustomed to elementary classrooms buzzing with curiosity, activity, and excitement, she asked me plaintively, "Where's the passion?" A difficult question to answer.

We did see high levels of activity in many vocational classrooms. Students and teachers suggested classrooms for us to visit. We saw some lively, exciting, and outstanding classrooms, but there were far too few exemplary classes.

It was fascinating to see the informal evaluation system that led us to the classrooms that both students and educators said were "the best" or "too good to miss." School personnel in several instances expressed surprise at how perceptive we were in discovering both what was strong and what was weak in a school, who the best teachers were, and what the problems were. It wasn't difficult—all we did was listen. When it came to agreement on who did an outstanding job of teaching, there was amazing accord. Teachers and students could not always explain their choices, but they did agree on who was "good." (Those who want a merit system based on some kind of measurement, take note.)

Students involved in the ASCD network were proud that their schools were part of such a project (although even in Scarsdale, which has repeatedly received national recognition, a student asked, "Is it really true that we're supposed to be good?"). They were proud to have a hand in helping to improve their schools. Gregg Krieger, Student Body President in San Rafael, spoke for many student leaders when he said:

> There were disturbances some years ago, but there's been quite a turnaround in the last few years. The students wanted a better school, and we worked on it. We feel good about our school now.

5 The Results Thus Far

A major study conducted by the Rand Corporation in the 1970s suggested that a large-scale project takes an average of three to five years to complete.[1] This finding also holds true for the ASCD project. Although a great deal has been accomplished already, most of the projects are continuing their work. Project accomplishments include increases in graduation requirements, more work in some subjects, less in others, and more requirements for seniors. However, network schools also developed their own schemes for organizing concepts, moved toward interdisciplinary teaching, and grappled with what to do with computers. Some changes were anticipated; others were not. There were constraints on what people wanted and plenty of criticism. People disagreed on the network's influence. All in all, the elaborate processes led to some equally elaborate and diverse results.

Increases in Graduation Requirements

A major result of the ASCD project is that many schools will increase the total number of specific courses required for graduation. Schools that are mandating these increases include not only those that empha-sized a reexamination of graduation requirements in the first place, such as Scarsdale, but also those, such as Pinellas Park, that spent a great deal of time defining outcome statements.

Once again, we need to point out that the ASCD study took place when state legislatures and countywide systems were examining these very same graduation requirements. As a result the California school systems, Ventura and San Rafael, made changes and saw these changes modified by California Senate Bill 813. The two school systems then added further modifications. Pinellas Park did not actively seek changes in graduation requirements, but several of the common learnings that it wanted to implement were done so automatically when the county mandated course additions in computer literacy, health, and the humanities. In addition to these changes, the Florida Legislature mandated three years of both mathematics and science for high school graduation.

With or without these outside influences, to date, seven of the network schools have moved to increase graduation requirements. Figure 11 summarizes changes these schools have made. In describing their graduation requirements, the schools use different counting systems. Some use semester hours; others use Carnegie units. Please note that only the major changes are described. Not included are proficiency examination requirements and many specific requirements in a discipline. For example, in Florida, social studies students are required to complete 30 hours of instruction in "Americanism vs. Communism."

Under the name of each system in Figure 11 we have listed both old requirements and new, the breakdown by subject-matter area, and the grand total of credits needed to graduate, subdivided into required courses and electives.

The redefinition process has led all seven of these schools to move to a larger core of required courses. Since both the California network schools and the state have mandated changes in graduation requirements, there are as many as three sets of requirements for students currently enrolled in the three California network high schools. To avoid confusion, we compared only the most recent requirements. However, the changes from the beginnings of the ASCD project until today are much more dramatic, since major additions have occurred in almost every area, including total number of required credits.

In Oak Park and Scarsdale, the total number of graduation credits has also been increased. Some schools have mandated that students do more work—an extra year in English, math, or science—while others are mandating specific courses in these fields. Previously, San Rafael required a year in any science; now it calls for a year of biological science and a year of physical science. Pinellas Park mandated four years of English/language arts. Each year will require a semester of grammar and composition and a semester of literature.

Figure 11. Graduation Requirement Changes

	Baltimore County		Oak Park[b]		Pinellas Park		San Rafael		Scarsdale		Ventura/ Buena	
	Old	New	Old	New	Old	New	Old	New	Old	New	Old	New
English/ language arts	4	4	3		3-1/2	4[d]	3	4	4	4	3-1/2	4
Social studies	4	4	2		2-1/2	3	2-1/2	3	3	3	3-1/2	3-1/2
Science	2	2	1		2	3	1	2[e]	1	2	1-1/2	2
Mathematics	2	3	1		2	3	2	2	1	2	1-1/2	2
Physical education	1	1-1/2	2	2	2	2	2-1/2				[h]	2
Foreign language								1[f]		1	1/2	1/2
Health		1/2	1/2			1/2	1/2	1/2	1/2	1/2		
Computers										1/2		
Consumer education			1/2									
Fine arts		1[a]		1[c]		1/2		1[f]			1	1
Practical arts				1-1/2		1/2				1/2	1	1
Communications				4								
Historical, cultural and global studies				4								
Math, science, and technology				4-1/2								
Required	13	16	10	17	12	16-1/2	11-1/2	14-1/2	9-1/2	13-1/2	12-1/2	16
Electives	7	4	9	3	10	7-1/2	10-1/2	7-1/2[g]	6-1/2	4-1/2	11-1/2	8
Total	20	20	19	20	22	24	22	22	16	18	24	24[i]

[a] One semester *each* of music and art is required.

[b] See material on page 92, which describes the Oak Park cluster concept.

[c] One credit in the fine *and* performing arts.

[d] One semester *each* of grammar-composition and literature is required each year.

[e] One year *each* of physical science and biological science is required.

[f] One year of foreign language *or* fine arts is required but not both.

[g] Meeting University of California entrance requirements reduces the number of electives a student can take to 4-1/2.

[h] A student had to be enrolled in Grades 9, 10, and 11, but no units were required.

[i] A full load is considered to be 24 credits, but to graduate a student must *pass* 22 credits.

Ames and the two Ann Arbor high schools may also add graduation requirements. Ames wanted to first fully develop its general education objectives and review what it was doing in its existing courses before even thinking about adding courses or increasing graduation requirements. Now that this process has been completed, Ames has discussed possible additions to report to its board of education in the spring of 1984.

Ann Arbor is also "in process" and will not be making any decisions about graduation requirements until at least the fall of 1984. In the proposals outlined in the "Green Book" were recommendations, for discussion purposes only, to require more course work in social studies, mathematics, and science and to add new requirements in the fine arts as well as in other areas. As had happened in the seven schools that have made their decisions, these proposals, if acted upon, would have decreased the number of electives and raised the number of required courses. These proposals suggest that one line of thinking in Ann Arbor is similar to that in the seven schools that have already made graduation changes.

Oak Park's Cluster Concept

One of the most interesting new patterns of requirements is the one adopted by Oak Park. It has moved from a more traditional curriculum approach to a board-approved cluster arrangement (Figure 12). The Oak Park faculty believed that the learning experiences they had defined as important might be taught in a number of different subject-matter courses and that many things that needed to be done transcended traditional subject-matter boundaries. For example, there was a strong belief that writing as a skill for lifelong learning needed improving; but the faculty at Oak Park also firmly believed that oral communication was important, too. The end result was a *communication cluster*. Initially, teachers felt that there should be a required oral communications course; but after further consideration they decided that a number of courses should be overhauled so that oral communications could be a part of each. In additon to six semesters of specified communications courses, each student must take two semesters of unspecified course work from a long list of approved communications courses, which may be housed in departments other

Figure 12. Oak Park and River Forest High School Graduation Requirements

The Clusters: All credits refer to a half year or semester.

Mathematics, Science, and Technology (9 credits)

Specified	4 mathematics
Specified	2 English
Specified	1 health education
Unspecified	2 credits freely chosen from the cluster

Communications (8 credits)

Specified	6 English
Unspecified	2 credits freely chosen from the cluster

Historical, Cultural, and Global Perspectives (8 credits)

Specified	2 American history
Specified	2 history
Unspecified	4 credits freely chosen from the cluster

Practical Arts (3 credits)

Specified	1 consumer education
Unspecified	2 credits freely chosen from the cluster

Fine and Performing Arts (2 credits)

Unspecified	2 credits freely chosen from the cluster

Physical Education (maximum: 4 credits)

Specified	1/2 credit (the value of one semester's work) for every semester a student attends school up through eight semesters

Driver Education

Specified	30 clock hours of classroom instruction

Figure 12. continued

Completing these requirements will yield a total of 34 credits. In addition to cluster credits, a student must take the equivalent of six more semester courses freely chosen, for a total of 40 credits for graduation. This set of requirements will ensure a student's exposure to a broader based general education.

To clarify which specific course titles will satisfy which cluster requirements, a sorting of course titles listed in the *Program of Studies* into cluster groups was completed. All courses are now in one cluster, and some courses are in two clusters but no more than two. Students must declare in which cluster they want a course to fulfill a requirement. A course cannot be used to fulfill the requirements in two different clusters.

than English, such as speech, foreign language, or business education.

In addition to the communications cluster, clusters have been created in mathematics, science, and technology; historical, cultural, and global perspectives; practical arts; and fine and performing arts. Students are also required to take a no-credit course in physical education each semester, except for one semester when they will take driver's education.

To date, all the courses taught in Oak Park have been sorted into the appropriate clusters, and a few courses have been trimmed. A reexamination of courses is under way to ensure that they do indeed receive the identified general education experiences that are appropriate to a cluster. This does not seem to be a particularly threatening situation to the faculty because there has been very little public criticism of courses. Board member Leah Marcus told us that there never has been much criticism because Oak Park never swung too far away from the traditional curriculum during the 1960s and 70s. Furthermore, we were told that most teachers were leaders in their fields. Physics teacher Joe Meyer, who was recently elected President of the American Physics Teachers Association (the first high school teacher to hold that position), is but one example of an outstanding record. Everyone involved was willing to change what needed changing, but there was no desire to change for the sake of change.

The cluster concept is interesting because it promotes a core curriculum and at the same time allows diversity within that core. In spite of the fact that Oak Park is experiencing an overall decline in enrollment, no department need feel that it will lose students, because all departments are represented in the core. Some courses may not thrive because students may not select them, and some faculty may need to be retrained; but, overall, Oak Park administrators felt they may need *more* teachers to meet the demands of the cluster program.

At the end of April 1984, Associate Principal Don Offerman reported the results of Oak Park's advanced fall registration. The new cluster requirements are meant to begin with the incoming fall 1984 9th grade class. However, an interesting phenomenon has developed. Students in 10th, 11th, and 12th grades apparently want to be as well prepared as the new 9th graders, so they, too, are signing up for the various cluster requirements. As a result, Oak Park may need to hire several teachers immediately. It is too early to generalize about this groundswell of support, but it certainly generates some interesting speculation about how willing some students are to improve the quality of their education.

Evidently, students see the benefits in this approach. They are given choice and diversity. "They don't have to eat pork, but they do have to eat something from the 'meat group' and something from the dairy family." To mix the metaphor, they don't eat at just one end of the table; they select from across the board. There's no attempt to homogenize everybody.

Increases in Subject-Matter Areas

Two of the big "winners" in the redefinition of required courses are mathematics and science. All seven schools now require two years of both science and mathematics, with Baltimore County requiring three years of mathematics. Given the external pressure from reformers, legislatures, and the public, this is no surprise. In several schools that are primarily college preparatory, such as Scarsdale, some teachers wondered if it was really worth all the effort to change the graduation requirements. "Ninety percent or more of the students are already taking two years of math and science, so what does this really mean?" (As an aside, a Scarsdale assistant superintendent said that only about

50 percent go beyond two years of science.) Increasing requirements doesn't necessarily lead to better teaching and education—"It's simplistic, and it doesn't solve any problems."

The response from those in Scarsdale who advocated and supported the increases was that we have "put our mouths and pens where our feelings are. It redefines the institution and should take care of graduation requirements for some time." Others added:

> This is comprehensive. We couldn't make decisions about the arts without looking at math and science as well.

If nothing else, this is a public confirmation that math and science are important and on a par with English.

But what will we teach students in schools that do not have a large college-preparatory population? These youngsters do not normally take two years of math and science. What should the curriculum be for these students? Do we water down courses in algebra or geometry? Do we add entirely new courses designed specifically for this group? Or do we simply let students take their chances and fail those who cannot make it?

Teachers continue to ponder these questions. Some are farther along because these issues were raised locally during the redefinition process. Others will need more time because they are working on recent state mandates. Pinellas Park, for example, had decided at the county level to move to two years of math and science; but the state has legislated three years of each. In the four schools that have not increased requirements in math and science or are not in the process of doing so, teachers think that it is only a matter of time before their state legislature or city administration pass similar requirements.

All of the schools that have increased their graduation requirements have moved to a requirement of four years in English/language arts/communications. This change was closely followed by a mandate for three to four years in the social sciences. Adding these requirements to the increases made in mathematics and science strongly suggests a network return to a core curriculum of the so-called "basics." A close examination of the learning outcomes that several schools developed serves to confirm this direction.

This move to strengthen basic skills has not been done at the expense of a balanced curriculum. In spite of all the talk about decreasing the amount of time spent in physical education, that subject seems to be holding its own. Baltimore has raised its requirement from one year to a year and a half, although San Rafael and Ventura have decreased the amount of time that will be spent in physical activity. Health has also held its place in most schools; and Oak Park, Pinellas Park, and Ventura have added requirements in the practical arts. The major addition to the curriculum has been in the fine arts/humanities. All seven schools have added a half-year or year requirement in this area.

Page High School, which has not changed its graduating requirements, has moved to implement a course in the humanities. [2] Several months ago the curriculum committee voted unanimously to reorganize an existing junior and senior level literature course with a humanities emphasis. Page teachers were pessimistic about the chances of this course being passed by the faculty. Recently we were told, "There was too much doom and gloom while you were here." Indeed there was. The faculty reviewed the existing course and expressed concern about a possible overemphasis on literature. With these concerns in mind, the English department began immediately to discuss the organization and content of the course. Fortunately, two members of the English department have a strong background in the humanities.

In January 1984 the Page School Board accepted the curriculum committee's proposal for the humanities course, which has been titled *The Spirited Human Expressions.* For the present the course will be a junior and senior elective. The whole process of looking at the humanities in Page has had the same impact that it has had elsewhere. Many staff members have been acutely awakened to a need for the humanities. Several now believe that the course should be required. Funds have been budgeted so that three staff members can develop the content of the course during the upcoming summer, and the school has applied for funding grants to help with staff development. The goal is to offer the course for the first time in the fall of 1984.

Ordinarily, this type of change does not enjoy the public constituency that the basics do. The latest *Phi Delta Kappan* Gallup Poll (September 1983) showed that only 16 percent of the public considers work in the humanities important. The faculties of at least eight of the network schools obviously disagree. Their thinking may have been influenced by Cawelti, Broudy, or others who have spoken at network meetings; in any event, they have decided that this area needs emphasis in the curriculum.

To date, San Rafael and Scarsdale are the only schools that have moved to make foreign languages a part of the required curriculum. San Rafael students have the choice of taking either one year of a foreign language or a year of fine arts. Scarsdale has decided to require one year of foreign language. Approximately 94 percent of Scarsdale students already take a language; nevertheless, the faculty feels that most students in the remaining 6 percent are also capable of taking a language. For those who may not be able to cope, a language course is offered in which the content is weighted more heavily with culture than it is with language. For a very few students even this requirement may be waived. Students whose native language is not English may choose between more work in English or a third language.

With the addition of several more mandated courses, the number of electives that a high school student can select has been cut back dramatically—anywhere from 30 percent to 66 percent. For college-bound students the degree of choice is even less because many will take three years of math and science plus a foreign language. Teachers and students are concerned that there may not be enough room to explore or make decisions about careers and/or fields of study.

Increases in Requirements for Seniors

Many schools hope that students will take even more courses, especially in their senior years. Teachers sometimes expressed the idea that the senior year is a waste of time for far too many pupils who are in a holding pattern until they graduate. The new graduation requirements should make this holding pattern a thing of the past.

To ensure that it does, Largo County in Florida, which includes Pinellas Park, has mandated that all seniors must attend school for six periods a day for a full year. Page does not allow early graduation, and Carlsbad requires students to apply a year before if they opt to graduate early. Oak Park students must take four credits a semester for all eight semesters. Ames offers chemistry to its seniors, including a double lab period.

Changes in Course Content

A major unfinished piece of business in many network high schools is to determine what course changes need to be made as a result of the redefinition process. To understand this need, we must review what has happened in several of the network schools.

The typical pattern in schools that developed outcome statements, as we have seen, was to define general education, select or develop a model to work from, spend many hours agreeing on an elaborate set of common learnings, and evaluate courses and/or change graduation requirements to strengthen the general education program. Six schools — San Rafael, Ames, Oak Park, Buena, Ventura, and Pinellas Park — have gone through this process. Pioneer and Huron are following the same path.

When major gaps were found, the first order of business was to change graduation requirements and/or add new courses. Page, for example, has added its new humanities course.

Several schools — Oak Park, Ames, Page, and Pinellas Park, for example — took elaborate inventories/surveys to determine to what degree the common learnings were being taught in the existing curriculum. Ames went a step beyond by trying to evaluate the quality of what was being done as well as the degree to which they were being taught. For these schools the task now is to make whatever changes are needed to see that the common learnings are taught, often adding concepts and skills on a course-by-course basis.

Because of its work, Ames has not yet added any new courses, although it may well increase graduation requirements in the near future. Instead, Ames wants to weave the desired concepts throughout the curriculum so that all students can be exposed to them. Several schools wondered if there is a logical sequence to the elements that make up the common learnings and, if so, how this sequence might be elaborated in a school's curriculum.

In examining their curriculum to see if the agreed-upon learning experiences were in evidence, the department heads in Oak Park discovered gaps. Art history, for example, emphasized Western art. Little was being done with non-Western art. The same was true in world history — strong emphasis on Western civilization, very little on the non-Western world. In the future, 25 percent of the world history course will reflect non-Western culture and history. According to Oak Park personnel, similar changes will be made in world literature and the humanities. The goal is to examine each cluster and each course to discover any gaps. Some type of monitoring will be required to ensure that every course fulfills its expectations, that every student will be exposed to the common learnings.

The two Ventura high schools spent a considerable amount of time identifying what should be taught to fulfill the goals defined for each of the six curriculum areas and the four branches of learning that make up their model. Courses are now being rewritten, and course sequences are being evaluated to ensure that each student is receiving instruction in the areas deemed critical by the Ventura staff. The goal is an integrated curriculum that reflects the four modes of teaching/learning (see Figure 9, p. 61) and one that will provide mastery in each goal area. Students and their parents will eventually know what minimal masteries are expected of each child.

Full implementation will probably take at least another year. Task forces will be working toward this goal during the summer of 1984. Currently, the English department, which has cut back considerably on electives, is totally rewriting its curriculum to fit into the general education model. A major question is, "How do we evaluate what we will be doing to ensure that students are really mastering the rewritten curriculum?" Bob Jones, Buena High School social studies teacher, felt that teachers will write common tests and observe one another to see how well things are developing. He saw school improvement and the redefinition of general education as inseparable and thought that the major result of the ASCD project will be that schools will reach more students, not just collectively, but also individually:

> We can expect students at all levels to write well. Advanced students will be able to do research and more complex writing. In reaching our goals, we'll make progress, but sometimes we will slip. The important point to keep in mind is what our goal is when the realities hit.

The need to examine what happens in courses and then to sequence them is especially urgent in Buena and Ventura High Schools because 9th grades in these cities have recently moved to the two high schools. The infusion of a large number of new teachers (according to one administrator, 20 percent of the faculty and 60 percent of the student body were new in 1983) has been a breath of fresh air, according to faculty members.

Ventura Principal Bob Cousar told us that his faculty, as part of their reexamination, agreed that the school's expectations for students have been too low and that the students should know what is expected of them. As a result, all students in all classes are given a *Statement of Success* (see Appendix D for several examples). Each statement outlines the basic objectives of the course, expectations for students academically and behaviorally, and grading policies. Students and their parents are asked to sign the document (in effect, a contract) so that everyone knows that the class is a serious undertaking. Cousar put it this way:

> School can be fun, but we want students to know that it isn't a game. We shouldn't sell kids short. I like Adler's idea [heard at a network meeting] that "the best education should go to all." We may have to lead or push, but the results can be so positive.

Cousar's dream is to expose students to some of the best of our cultural heritage—especially in opera.

San Rafael Principal Steve Collins supported this view. San Rafael, like several other schools, is looking at course content. One new option will be either a one-year course in foreign language or the humanities. To further ensure that all students have the opportunity to enrich themselves culturally, San Rafael has launched a creative arts program, in which diverse performers regularly visit the school. Teachers must sign up to take their students to these performances, which occur twice a month during the school day. Before the event, teachers prepare their students for the program, which is considered part of the total curriculum. The emphasis is on learning to be a good audience and appreciating a performance, whatever it might happen to be. Fund raising helps pay for these events, although many are free. Others are funded by the Buck Foundation, a local philanthropic organization.

Principal Eloise Lee, a recent arrival at Denver's East High, hopes to use this year's two and one-half days for curriculum development to evaluate what has been accomplished. She would like to start by identifying sequential competencies in mathematics. In the past East High School has tried a number of experimental courses. Lee hopes that variety will not be lost if Denver cuts the number of courses from approximately 500 to 350, as has been predicted.

The 105 common learnings helped Pinellas Park to focus on which teachers were actually teaching as well as what they should teach. Currently, the faculty must reconcile the common learnings with the new county requirements in the humanities, health, and computer literacy. The humanities and health requirements (1/2 credit each) will fit nicely with common learnings that were not being taught. The county is now developing a computer literacy unit that will probably be inserted into a science course. The identified common learnings may still not be met, however, because some students may not enroll in this designated course. Meeting the common learnings is still a concern in Pinellas Park.

Interdisciplinary Teaching

All of these schools have continued to work on the reconciliation of common learnings with what now goes on in courses. Obviously, this process will continue for some time. An immediate result is that it has led teachers in several schools to regard teaching and curriculum organization along lines that are far more interdisciplinary than ever before. During our interviews this trend came as something of a surprise. ASCD had asked the schools, in writing their final reports, to use a five-point scale to rate "the extent to which interdisciplinary teaching has resulted." Of the ten schools that responded, nine gave a "2" rating, and one gave a rating of "1," overall a very low response. The key words, we discovered, were "has resulted." To date there has not been widespread change (active interdisciplinary teaching); but there is, nevertheless, much sentiment for such a move and/or much discussion about what might be done. For example, the steering committee and department chairpersons in Pinellas Park told us that thinking about common learnings led teachers in different departments to realize that they were teaching to common ends. When the common learnings did not always fit neatly under specific headings, their response was to discard the headings:

> The more we did, the more we realized how connected education is, how interdisciplinary it is.

Committee members in Ames, Denver, and Oak Park agreed. In Denver we heard,

> This whole process has given us a fresh look at education. It has helped to bring the threads together, to show how the various subjects relate to one another. We have been teaching with blinders, looking only at our own areas.

Teachers in Ames and Oak Park felt that they were forcing themselves to think along interdisciplinary lines. In Oak Park, several committee members believed that in creating the concept of clusters they had overcome the departmentalization of knowledge. They felt that their departments will function under newly self-imposed pressures to revise and combine courses, to look at interdisciplinary work. As an example, the science department head told us that his department will begin integrating new learnings into science; for instance, assigning oral reports to his chemistry students. "If this trend doesn't lead to interdisciplinary teaching, it's got to lead to *something* that's more connected." As another teacher put it, "There's more to math in math than math."

Several teachers in the larger schools believed that departments had kept faculties isolated. In some schools teachers are fortunate enough to have either departmental offices or individual offices in which they can do their work. (In Scarsdale, most departments have a secretary as well.) There may no longer be a faculty room; but even if there was one, most teachers would not spend much time there because they prefer to work in their offices. This is somewhat of a mixed blessing. Teachers realize that individual faculty offices foster isolation and may break down the new communication. "People just don't get together." On the other hand, most teachers quickly added, "Death to him who tries to take away our offices!"

In Page, we were told that interdepartmental communication is not a problem. The faculty is small, and people frequently cross department lines to teach — vocational education teachers teach science, and so on. Thus, there is greater cooperation.

The move toward interdisciplinary teaching was by no means limited to schools that had developed common learnings. According to Principal Bob Gaut, the faculty at O. Perry Walker recognized a need to consider what was going on in other subjects. As a result, two new broad-based departments have been created. Business, industrial arts, and home economics have been combined into the applied arts department; and art, music, and drama have been combined into the cultural arts department.

In Scarsdale, teachers and department chairs told us that the ASCD project had caused them to think about interdisciplinary teaching. A few felt that the departments were still too much in their own "little fiefdoms." We were also told repeatedly that "this faculty thinks along subject-matter lines." Most faculty members earned their master's degrees, and several earned their doctorates, in subject-matter fields and are very active in those fields; they write books, give presentations before professional organizations, and work with groups such as the College Entrance Examination Board. The department heads believed this professional involvement is a major reason that Scarsdale is such a stimulating place in which to work.

Regardless of what exists now, there is definitely a move toward the interdisciplinary in Scarsdale. In the next school year (1984-85), three new interdisciplinary courses will be available — one entitled *Male/Female*, a joint English-social studies venture, and two other courses with combined subject matter: physics and social studies, and literature and art. Also, as a direct result of the ASCD project, planning is under way for a staff development program on interdisciplinary teaching. The administration said that this teaching will probably cause a scheduling nightmare; however, it will probably decrease faculty isolation.

The Place of the Computer

In redefining general education in the American high school, we cannot ignore the computer revolution. Although computer-assisted instruction, programming, and other computer-related instruction have been in schools for several years, all have shown varying degrees of success. Until recently, all were tied to large, expensive main frame computers. What is new is the explosion of interest in relatively low priced micro-computers, which makes it possible for home and school to have access to ever more sophisticated machines and programs. The major problem for the high school lies in deciding where best to include computers in the curriculum.

Computers were used in every school we visited. Carlsbad High School runs four awareness classes and four programming classes (BASIC). They also use computers in some business courses. Buena High School hopes to move computers into the 9th grade curriculum. And so it was from school to school.

The mathematics curriculum (followed by science and business) is "home" for more computers than any other area. Pioneer High School uses 30 to 40 computers to teach math, science, and business in both classrooms and in a computer laboratory. The computer program in mathematics at Pioneer has been cited by the National Institute for Education as an exemplary program, one of only two or three in the country that truly integrates computer-assisted instruction into mathematics teaching.

Across town, Huron High School has a hybrid lab that includes a main frame plus several micro-computers provided by the board of education. Their short-term goal is to assign every mathematics student some work on computers. Science students are working in this lab, but math is the core subject. Business education intends to have its own lab as soon as possible. Students can work in the lab during their study halls; hence, the lab facility is heavily used. The major problem here, and in many American high schools, is insufficient faculty to staff the lab during every period.

Throughout the network there was by no means a consensus that computers "belonged" in math, science, and business. We heard several variations on a statement attributed to David Lloyd George and Georges Clemenceau, "War is much too serious a matter to be entrusted to the military." The contemporary version is that computers are far too serious a matter to be entrusted to mathematics teachers. To date, Scarsdale is the only school to mandate a half-year in computers for all students and to add two new teachers to work in the program. Even now before this requirement has gone into effect, several hundred students are enrolled in computer courses. New computers have been purchased, and teachers are being given time and pay to work on the program.

At least three schools are developing computer education programs that will touch as many subject-matter courses as possible. As mentioned earlier, Oak Park intends to teach and use computers throughout the curriculum and to that end is providing its faculty with the prerequisite training. O. Perry Walker has already added a computer literacy course and, as a result of the ASCD project, has established a school Computer Center that will be used in several academic courses.

A fortuitous calamity has helped Buena High School to build one of the most comprehensive computer programs in southern California. For many years the keystone of the program was one large computer that had, unfortunately, outlived its usefulness. When this white elephant was stolen from the school, the faculty were stunned. But they quickly turned adversity into opportunity by applying their insurance money (and new funds, which they quickly raised) toward a mini-computer and 32 terminals as well as several micro-computers and word processors. With this hardware, the school will be able to provide computer contact to a majority of students in a wide range of subjects. One cannot help but wonder what would happen if the thief or thieves were to come forward: five to 10 years in jail *and* a school distinguished service award!

Exposure or Mastery

At the network's last meeting in Vail, Colorado, in July 1983, the assembled leaders were asked how much schoolwide testing was necessary to find out if the curriculum elements (courses, common learnings, new graduation requirements, or whatever) that their schools had deemed important were actually being taught and learned. At the time, there were considerable differences of opinion among the leaders. Paul Rosier of Page, Arizona, reported that his teachers challenged their administrators, "Ask us to do one of two things: teach *or* test and keep records." On the other side of the issue, Ben Ebersole of Baltimore County pointed out, "In districts with 20 high schools, the board wants to know what's happening in Algebra I. [3] At the end of the Vail meeting, the question, "Do the network schools want their students to be exposed to the major learnings, or are they moving to mastery learning?" remained largely unanswered. Hence, we were asked to raise the question as we visited each of the network schools.

We heard a variety of responses. A steering committee member in Denver challenged whether the question involved an 'either/or' situation. "It's neither competency nor exposure. It's a continuum." As he saw it, a teacher exposes a student to learning and then strives to take the student to the highest level of competency that the student can handle. In Page, we were told that competency ("as far as the kids can go") is the goal in many areas; but in the new humanities course, the emphasis will be on exposure. In several schools we were told:

> The state will have an influence in the long run on the answer to that question, but for now we can only answer that exposure is what we want in these areas because a few months ago we didn't have anything. Mastery, if a goal at all, is a goal that we will reach in the future.

In California, San Rafael High School and both Ventura schools were the most adamant about intending to move toward mastery in the near future. They need and want a system of evaluation. At Buena High, school personnel said:

> We're in a whole new process. We need an evaluation system to ensure that the kids get the things we said they ought to get.

Furthermore, California Senate Bill 813 mandated that every school in the state set "Standards of Public Achievement"; that is, testing and evaluation must be established by December 1984. Baltimore County seems headed in the same direction through a coordinated countywide and local school testing program.

Two schools disagreed on their goals but agreed on a method to see whether or not the curriculum is being taught. Oak Park was the only school reporting that it had "unabashedly gone for exposure rather than mastery." Oak Park is a district that believes in testing sparingly. It uses a minimal competency test as a diagnostic tool to screen youngsters who need help. Oak Park obtains a writing sample from every student as a freshman and later as a junior and then compares the two to see how much progress the student has made. Ames, on the other hand, is emphasizing exposure for the time being, but felt that exposure is not enough; mastery will be the long-term goal. Oak Park felt that courses have their own unique levels of mastery and evaluation and that what is necessary is a monitoring system to ensure that the common learnings are being taught. Ames agreed with this need for monitoring.

Ames Superintendent of Schools Paul Masem argued that monitoring is a major management information tool. Programs may fail because they are not conceptually sound; but programs also fail because, quite simply, they are not implemented. He cited an example concerning quantitative data collected on a new elementary program in a district where he had previously worked. Test results showed that one group of students was not doing well in the new program, but the results gave no hint as to why. By monitoring the program and interviewing the program teachers, he discovered that three teachers had failed to teach a critical part of the program. For one reason or another, they had missed the inservice training necessary to teach the new program. Lacking this skill, they continued to teach the old program instead of the new one. After Masem arranged training for these teachers, he noted that student test scores shot up dramatically within a short period of time.

This is not an unusual story. What *is* unusual is that the problem was discovered. Another unusual aspect is that the curriculum was not labeled a failure; rather, the problem was rectified. Monitoring, as Masem saw it, is an important formative evaluation tool that helps administrators to make mid-course corrections, to see firsthand what is happening. Ames Assistant Superintendent Luther Kiser added that effective monitoring should be continuous. To that end, Ames has added a staff person with a background in curriculum and instruction as well as in evaluation to establish an ongoing monitoring system.

Faculty Sense of Accomplishment

To discover what the faculty in the network schools felt they had accomplished, we asked as many people as possible, "What are the highlights of what you have done? What have you accomplished?"

Here are some representative answers:

Buena: The *process!* Make sure you tell people that the product is not nearly as important as the process.

Scarsdale: Emphasize that this is an educating *process.*

Pinellas Park: The best thing is that this project made us look at ourselves. This was an examination of conscience. It made us look at what we were doing.

Carlsbad: The big thing was that it got people to think about curriculum.

No other question we asked aroused so much emotion. It didn't take us long to understand why. Below are more comments heard from the various schools.

Pinellas Park: The process made our jobs seem of consequence.

Ames: We found that we need each other.

Buena: It was a big confidence builder. This was a real soul searching. We feel very good about the staff's awareness. The process made us conscious of things that we hadn't thought about.

East High: We've had more discussion of curriculum and issues than in any previous year in recent history

O. Perry Walker: Teachers got a more global view of education. We broke out of our own disciplines and got started thinking about what a high school should be.

Ames: Teachers teaching the same course worked together.

Pinellas Park: We got a clearer idea of what we were doing in our own classes and what others are doing in their classes. It opened communication among teachers and departments.

A systematic approach to the evaluation and development of curriculum aroused strong feelings. The Ventura School District emphasized these feelings in its final report:

Ventura Unified School District takes the position that far more important than any specific written document is the process employed in developing the document, because it is the process which will truly determine action, not the document.

Schools were proud of the fact that, as Ames Principal Ralph Farrar asserted, "What we have been doing is a reaction to needs rather than a reaction to trends and national hysteria over reports such as *A Nation at Risk.*" Individual teachers, especially steering committee members, told us repeatedly that the project had made a difference in their own teaching. In Denver, for example, we heard, "If nothing else, here are eight people (the steering committee members) who are better teachers than they were before."

It was exciting to talk to people who zealously maintained this position throughout the project's highs and lows. Many were true believers who hoped other systems would try the same process. Several administrators felt that more than ever before their faculties were open to thinking about change, that morale was often higher but frequently accompanied by disillusionment when the faculty saw how long it took to effect change.

After listening to teachers and administrators talk about the process, we probed to find out what else they thought they had accomplished. As expected, we heard much talk about the specifics of the models, the common learnings, and new graduation requirements. We also found that there were other accomplishments, some of which went beyond the consideration of general education.

In Baltimore, a teacher commented, "What we do is usually not dramatic." Yet the Baltimore County Board of Education was so impressed with the changes that came out of the ASCD project that they authorized 44 new positions and allowed the system to keep an additional 45 positions that would have been lost due to declining enrollments. As a direct outgrowth of the general education model, the Baltimore County study group developed a Baltimore County Achievement Program. This program seeks to acknowledge the academic excellence achieved by outstanding students who complete a rigorous program of 24 credits (16 general education and 8 electives) in designated areas of concentration—liberal arts, science/technology, and vocational education. Students must maintain at least a "C" average. Those who maintain a "B" average will receive a special seal of merit attached to their Certificates of Achievement. The Woodlawn Dimensions committee has elaborated on this program by creating a 26-credit program and Certificate of Achievement in general liberal arts, general vocational/trade industry, mathematics, science, business, and physical education.

Educators at East High School in Denver believed that as a result of the ASCD process they have a head start over other city high schools in the inevitable changes yet to come because of the work accomplished by the steering committee and faculty. East High has also reviewed its vocational courses and has considered changes in addition to those already discussed.

Schools frequently listed very specific accomplishments. O. Perry Walker has reorganized its schedule so that most department members share a common planning time, which facilitates open discussion among teachers. Committee members felt that as a result of the hard look they took at the curriculum and course content, the faculty has become more aware than ever of the importance of courses such as the humanities, foreign languages, and creative writing. They are "more noticeably willing to consider course revision and implementation." This awareness and the processes that they used—debate, committee meetings, quality circle discussions, and others—have resulted in a Recommended Model Curriculum (see Figure 13), which may be recommended to the board of education, depending on the actions of the Louisiana state legislature, which is considering changes in graduation requirements.[4]

Figure 13. O. Perry Walker's Recommended Model Curriculum

Language Arts:
   Speech
   Journalism
	—	4 years

Mathematics	—	3 years
Science	—	2 years
Social Studies	—	3 years (one more than required by the state)
Physical Educaton	—	2 years

Fine Arts:
   Art
   Music
   Drama
   Humanities
		1 year (one more than required
		   by the state)

Applied Arts:
   Industrial Arts
   Home Economics
   Business Subjects
   Computer Electronics/
   Science
	—	1 year (one more than required
		   by the state)

Total	—	16 units

Please note that Louisiana students must now earn 13-1/2 required units out of a total of 22. This leaves a total of 6 additional units, which can be selected from most of the areas mentioned above.

The state board for higher education has recommended that high school graduates attempt 24 units and pass 22 to graduate. They are apparently concerned about the "early release" syndrome and feel all students need more preparation before leaving high school.

Apparently, the Walker faculty feels the same way. Our recommendation adds 2-1/2 units to the general education block.

Carlsbad has moved certain activities (for example, the Student Council and cheerleading) outside the regular school day and has cut back on vocational education. Currently, committees are designing a program that will increase the faculty's capacity to counsel and advise students.

Page has already begun a teacher advisory system to help students and parents understand the paths and choices available to each youngster. So far, 50 percent of the parents have been involved in personal conferences with teacher advisors, a percentage that will grow because the board has mandated that all students and their parents must participate in such conferences. Principal Paul Rosier felt that the procedure is already showing positive results. The number of students going on to college is at an all-time high, and the number of sections of algebra has risen from two to six. Also, fewer students are now marking time in an undefined program; more have actually signed up for vocational education or a college preparatory program. The number of business education students, for example, has doubled.

Unanticipated Outcomes

We asked faculty members if they had experienced any unanticipated outcomes, anything that had not shown up in their reports to ASCD. The most frequent answers concerned *support* and *time:*

> We were pleased at how much public support we got. We weren't sure we would get any!

> It was obvious that the community wanted to see the project accomplished.

> We got lots of press coverage.

> It looks like this community wants to see the school have more control over education.

> We were really surprised at how little opposition there was.

Others were happy at how well things had progressed but were surprised at how long everything took. O. Perry Walker committee member Ethel Istre spoke for people from many project schools:

> We never envisioned the scope of the project. The enormity of it didn't hit us until much later. Every time we did something, we saw there was something more to do.

One administrator confided that he sometimes felt threatened when people complained, "We said we were going to do this, so why haven't we?" He felt he was trying but that the real power was at a higher level.

There were also some highly specific unanticipated outcomes. Page High School's new Computer Lab was a direct result of the ASCD project. Ames discovered that several of its elementary and middle school principals realized that their schools would also have to look at their programs. "To start at the high school level," they felt, "is really an example of the tail wagging the dog. *All* grade levels have to examine what it is they are doing." To help this process, Ames High School Principal Ralph Farrar has explained the ASCD project to his elementary and middle school administrative colleagues.

Leadership Changes

With all the curriculum changes that were being made in the network as a result of the ASCD process, we wondered if there were also changes being made in the area of school leadership. For example, we have already mentioned the addition of a research person at the district level in Ames.

We did not find very many changes. An impressive change, though, involved Douglas Lynn, a prime mover in the Carlsbad project. His position was upgraded from one that was half-time as assistant principal and half-time as a dean to a full-time position as assistant principal. In Oak Park, Associate Principal Don Offerman is now responsible for anything concerning curriculum and instruction. This change was made because the school's efforts had been too decentralized.

Page now has an assistant principal for research, who is responsible for documenting student progress. Page would like to conduct a five-year follow-up study to obtain specific information on the results of their efforts.

The other network schools did not report any major changes. Responsibilities were added to existing jobs, and several principals indicated that department heads would be asked to do more curriculum work in the future. One principal, who lost his department heads in a major financial crunch, would like to redefine the position and institute the position of instructional leader, which he feels could be invaluable. Page's Paul Rosier said that he has partially redefined his own position as a result of the ASCD experience. To keep the lines of communication open, he now meets separately with each department at least twice a year.

And Now a Word from Our Curmudgeon and Other Critics

In an attempt to make sure that we heard the other side of the story, something beyond the latest refrain of "Everything's Coming Up Roses," we asked project school administrators, "How would your faculty curmudgeon react to what you have done and to what has happened?" We also asked a number of faculty members, as well as the administrators, to direct us to this faculty curmudgeon, so that we could speak to him or her directly. These delightful conversations— always direct, never ill-tempered, always candid—provided us with highly interesting information. In addition, several who were strong supporters of the project voiced their reservations about what their schools had done or how they had done it. As you will see, several felt that certain issues had not been addressed that should have been.

Very few of our curmudgeons were totally opposed to the project, although one or two did resign from the steering committee because they did not want to see the proposed changes take place. The feeling seemed to be, "We're already good, so we don't have to change." This was a relatively rare stance. A far more commonly held belief was, "We put lots of time into this project and I'm not sure it was all worth it; we got too bogged down." Or if things had gone well the attitude was,

> Let's wait and see what happens with the rest of what we do. So far we have merely redefined, which isn't anything really new. Now we have to see if there's any follow-through.

In a number of schools people questioned whether teachers had been sufficiently involved in the process. A fellow teacher voiced the opinion that when it came to trying to change, too many of his colleagues "had seen 'em come and seen 'em go."

We've seen so many things come down the pike that some people don't want to try anything new. Nobody ever follows through, and we're left with another stalled bandwagon. At least, *A Nation at Risk* has focused our attention on the fact that there are problems in our schools that have to be addressed.

Another teacher in the same school believed that nothing much had happened in the project. He felt that this type of project should be aimed at the teachers in the middle.

You're not going to help the poor ones; aim at the ones in the middle. First you've got to find out what the kids need and then make the teachers conscious of these needs so they can work to fulfill them in the way they want to. There are many ways to approach a goal like this, not just one.

The most thoughtful skepticism was reserved for the outcomes, be they common learnings or graduation requirement changes. A Denver teacher insisted that one common learning should be for every student to learn to swim. Several teachers in Page wanted a new course that went beyond driver's education (which every student does not take) to include a knowledge of survival automobile maintenance. This course suggestion might seem odd to people living in more populous areas, but it makes sense in northern Arizona. This course was not adopted, but it seemed to be practical learning. It raised a question in my mind, "Do we do enough with common learnings unique to a given population or environment?" Are we making a mistake if we try to homogenize our ideas of what we want all teenagers to learn 'to the least common denominator'?

A Denver mathematics teacher questioned why we do not teach our young people how to become successful in life, "to give them the skills to deal with people and to sell themselves." Others asked, "What about mental health? Where does it fit in? And how about understanding the passages in life?" Recalling the period 1964-1983, during which teenage suicides increased by 300 percent, I wondered, too.

Others asked, "In raising graduation requirements are we becoming too dictatorial and imposing too much of a lockstep in the curriculum?" "It's going to be as it was when we were kids. There aren't enough options left," was the comment of an over-40-year-old teacher. "Where do learning styles fit in?" queried another. "We're pushing the poorer students to drop out of school" was the fear of several teachers.

Another frequent comment was:

> Making it harder is not making it better. If we don't improve our
> teaching, too, we haven't made any gains. We've only raised the hurdles.

Teachers worried, "What are we going to take out if we keep on
adding? We can't finish all that we do now." Another added, "Individual teachers have their students for one hour a day. How many
miracles can they work?"

In only one school was there a formal "Graduation Requirements
Committee Minority Opinion." Written by the head librarian and the
head guidance counselor at Scarsdale High School, this opinion was
included as an integral part of Scarsdale's final report. The co-authors
judged that the review process was a good one; however, like several
other teachers in Scarsdale and the other network schools, they
believed that increasing graduation requirements in and of itself
would not lead to better teaching or better learning. It is a simplistic
solution to a complex problem; and it sends the message that if
students want a good education, all they need to do is take so many
units of this and so many units of that. This does not help students, in
particular, disaffected students. By "disaffected" these teachers meant
"teenagers who for psychological reasons live fairly marginal lives as
children." Increasing graduation requirements does not develop a
real love of learning. The real issue is "how to get young people to
want to be educated. Let us look instead to course content, to the
variety of our offerings, and to the kind of learning environment we
believe will best foster growth and discovery and creativity." This
eloquent message evoked considerable support in Scarsdale and in
other network schools as well.

In discussing their views on the ASCD project with people in the
network schools, we expected to hear comments about recent reports
critical of the American high school and also about the recent actions
of several state legislatures to mandate new graduation requirements.
Opinions were mixed concerning the national reports. Some recommendations that sprang from these reports were seen as flights of
fancy that would have little impact on the schools. Nevertheless, many
teachers were "glad that education was in the spotlight again rather
than on the back burner." Oak Park board member Leah Marcus, a
strong supporter of Oak Park's project, believed that the issue in the

reports is really "schooling vs. learning." The national reports emphasize formal, institutionalized schooling; and they assume that by increasing the quantity of schooling, the result will be more and better
learning. Like so many others, she wondered if this is a valid assumption.

Many network teachers were angry about state-mandated increases
in graduation requirements. "The people who write the bills have no
idea of what goes on in a classroom." Others called the state actions
"upgrading education with a sledge hammer," and in requiring three
years of math and science, "legislating failure." One teacher called
them "et cetera bills."

> The state passes a sweeping mandate, *etc.,* and in effect says, "We'll get
> around to the et ceteras later on." My major concern is that nothing is
> ever said about the quality of what we are supposed to do.

Opinions varied from state to state. In states where school personnel had the chance to voice their opinions, or were given some sense
of direction and some help to reach the new state goals, the criticisms
were somewhat muted. But in at least one state, there was near
unanimous agreement that the message in the new state mandate was,
"You haven't put your house in order so we're going to do it for you."
Teachers deeply resented this message, along with the fact that the
state's high school personnel had virtually no chance to speak on the
new changes.

Administrators, as well as teachers, worried about the rush to
mandate more and more state or local requirements, with neither a
thorough examination of what is needed nor a report of what is being
done to improve (for instance, the network projects). One administrator wondered how students will ever become self-directed and independent thinkers in "a mandated learning environment"; however, he
also said, "You've got to get aboard, or even more conservative forces
are going to run the movement."

In five network communities, teachers and administrators sounded
a critical message for parents: parents must be held accountable for
the education of their children. But it was a parent at East High in
Denver who summarized it best:

> Education is not just the school's responsibility. Parents need to know
> this. For example, reading starts with the young child. If they don't learn

then, you can't apply a Band-Aid in high school. It's too late. To get a good school, parents, teachers, and administrators have to work together—Right is Right; Wrong is Nobody.

Several schools observed that parents become involved when it's time to start college planning, but at other times they rarely take part in decision making. School personnel know that these are difficult times for closer school/family ties: the divorce rate is high; there are many single parent homes and many latchkey students. As a result, several teachers and administrators told us that they think parents have lower expectations for their children. What was needed, one Oak Park parent observed, was "to cultivate the ardent parent!" But how is this done?

On one point everyone seemed to agree—an involved parent is a formidable asset. Where parents were active participants in the redefinition process, they were usually viewed as priceless treasures. "If only we had more," was a common faculty refrain.

On the lighter side, Bill Loess, Carlsbad school board member and former Carlsbad High School principal, cautioned about longing too much for the good old days.

> I've heard so many people say how much better kids used to do in math and the other subjects; and, you know, I had many of these people as students when they were younger, so I questioned this. Finally, I decided to look in our old school records and see just how well some of these people had done when they were young. I found that most of them didn't do any better than our students do today.

Amusing, but Loess felt there was a serious message, too. Students from poor families used to fall by the wayside, but now they stay in school. "We've become more concerned, but we can't expect miraculous changes. Schools will only be as good as society insists they be. If we are not willing to sacrifice [to make the schools better], we can't expect the kids to do more."

Implementation

The ASCD project is officially over, but that does not mean that the 14 network schools have completed their self-imposed processes and tasks. Although it remains to be seen how many schools will continue without the motivation and sponsorship of the network, the evidence

from the interviews is that all but three or four of the schools will
continue to develop and implement their redefinition process for
another two or three years. At least half of the schools are still going
strong and, indeed, will resent any implication that they might not see
their projects through to completion. In these schools the fact that the
network has ended is of little consequence since the project has a
strong local life of its own.

Specifically, the two Ventura high schools estimated that the project
will take two to three years to complete. Ames surmised that it will take
three, and Carlsbad estimated that full implementation will not come
until 1985-86. Oak Park, which will begin the first stage of implementation—instituting the cluster concept in 1984-85—projected another
four years after the first stage to apply the new requirements to all
students. As we have seen, the Ann Arbor Schools have redefined their
schedule and will continue to work toward this goal. San Rafael said
that redefinition is an ongoing process, and administrators at O. Perry
Walker felt that they had just scratched the surface. Since the redefinition process is such a broad topic, they wondered if they will ever be
able to tackle all the issues! For example, what about the affective
issues? School climate? And so on.

Of all the schools only Pinellas Park believed that they will finish at
the building level during the current school year. However, at the
county and state levels, Assistant Superintendent of Secondary Education Kenneth Webster will ensure that the Pinellas Park common
learnings are made available to all county high schools. A workshop
will be held for all principals, assistant principals, and supervisors to
make them aware of what has been done. This information will also be
shared with statewide groups and organizations in the coming months
so that by the fall of 1984, Pinellas Park's common learnings will be
disseminated across the state of Florida.

Staff Development

Staff development will be a major emphasis in the coming months
in several project schools. As an administrator at Huron High School
pointed out:

> Everyone realizes that there will be a need for a lot of staff development
> so that the changes we are making can be wisely implemented.

Buena High will deliberately phase in its program gradually so that teachers can get retraining if needed.

As mentioned, Oak Park will conduct inservice workshops to ensure that oral communication is improved throughout the curriculum. According to Associate Principal Don Offerman,

> We need staff development. It's a key to our success, and it helps to keep our staff alive.

Members of the Oak Park steering committee agreed:

> We feel good that we are implementing what we have done and that the work is continuing, but we now need staff development. A separate committee will work with teachers to improve instruction. This is not a project where work is done and then tucked away in a drawer. This is only a beginning.

In addition, members of the steering committee also believed that the ASCD project had been an outstanding effort in staff development.

> As committee members, we changed a lot. In talking and working with other people outside our committee, we became something more than just friends and colleagues. There was a spider web effect, and it created a tighter faculty.

When it decides on the recommendations that it wants to make, Carlsbad High School will send its results to a districtwide accrediting committee, which will review them before they are sent to the superintendent and board of education. This committee was set up to ensure better scope and sequence in the Carlsbad K-12 curriculum.

Scarsdale has announced that it wants to encourage staff development on interdisciplinary teaching. The vehicle to reach this goal is a unique agency, The Scarsdale Teachers' Institute. Founded by the board of education, the Institute is run by a teacher who is released half-time to schedule staff development opportunities that respond first and foremost to faculty needs (not necessarily those of the school administration). The coordinator's job is to propose staff development experiences, whatever they may be, and then to hire people to teach them. The instructors may or may not be Scarsdale faculty members. The Institute, as a direct result of the ASCD project, is now establishing a program on interdisciplinary teaching. According to several department chairs, 55-60 percent of the Scarsdale faculty are involved in taking courses through the Institute. To encourage this kind of staff development, the Scarsdale board of education has added an *MA + 75 hours* step to the salary schedule. A Scarsdale teacher commented:

> It's things like this that make Scarsdale such an attractive place to work. There are several schools in the area where the salaries are better, but the working conditions here are great.

The Board of Education

To date, two thirds of the project schools have made either formal presentations or have asked for and received formal board approval for the changes they were seeking. For the future, leaders in most of the network schools strongly suggested that the board be kept up to date on what is happening in the project at all times. Page, for example, sent a board member to every network meeting.

It was more difficult to keep people up to date in some of the larger systems; nevertheless, it is very important. The process worked in Baltimore, where the board has approved the various recommendations for change. In Oak Park, a much smaller district than Baltimore, the board of education, after listening for two years to what was happening and to what was proposed, voted unanimously to pass the recommended changes. In most of the districts that have not yet made their final recommendations, the goal is to seek a vote within the next two years.

Constraints in the Schools

The project schools were asked to report what constraints or other factors existed as barriers to their anticipated progress and to list any other forces that operated during the life of the project that perhaps weighed more heavily on the status of general education than the ASCD project. Ventura's final report noted that it did not see these forces as necessarily negative ones but that they did have an impact and in most cases did represent a reduction of staff resources.

Eight schools reported that two factors were especially important: (1) budget restrictions/money problems, and (2) restrictions because of existing state curriculum requirements and/or new legislation concerning graduation requirements.

Whether they were called "budget restraints," "major shortfalls," "reduction of allocated funds," or "funding difficulties," it was obvious that several of the districts had problems finding the money "to work with their models," "to buy materials," to "facilitate implementation in the classroom," indeed, to implement what they had accomplished in all its facets. For example, no state has seen a more dramatic change in its financial affairs in recent years than California. According to information given us by California principals, the percent of income spent on schools in California is now the lowest in the country. We were told that in actual dollars California is spending $2,100 per pupil, or about $1,000 per pupil less than the neighboring state of Oregon. California now also has the highest average class size in the nation. All of this is a result of Proposition 13, which has shifted funding (with a corresponding loss of local control) from the local level to the California legislature.

Not all of the financial problems were a result of districts' inability to tax themselves. In several network schools, people questioned the fairness of equalization formulas. "We could spend more on education, but the state won't let us," or "With a special vote we can spend 10 percent more than the formula, but that's all." No one questioned the fairness of a strong minimum, but teachers and administrators alike asked if it is fair to hold back districts where the community is willing to spend more to educate the children.

Many state legislatures have recently tied funding to reforms—such as increased graduation requirements and lengthened school days. Thus, it becomes more and more difficult for reform-minded school districts to take local action. Even where there has not been new legislation, the network schools have had problems in meeting existing standards that may impede their progress. State guidelines on vocational education, special education, and a number of other areas are part of this problem.

People in Pinellas Park felt that the number of changes or proposed changes—stiffer math and science graduation requirements, a longer school day, merit pay, Proposition I (Florida's yet-to-be-voted-on answer to Propositon 13), the Florida Sate Commission on Education, and others—makes student counseling and local planning somewhat difficult. Some teachers felt that the results of their efforts would have to be put on the back burner until the picture was a lot clearer. As in other states, a number of teachers saw attacks on education as being a popular activity among politicians. Not everyone agreed with this opinion, either in Florida or in the other states; on the other hand, there are many who do.

Personnel changes and school schedules were important constraints for at least four schools. People left the steering committees; teachers moved into administration; or key administrators who had been supportive either moved up or out, interrupting the flow of progress. A Denver teacher reminded us,

> Don't forget the busing theory of curriculum development—you can only do what can be accommodated by the bus schedule.

Approaching Page for our visit, we saw students disembarking their school buses at the end of the school day, and we were still an hour away from Page, a situation we were told is not unusual in Arizona. In Pinellas Park, 95 percent of the high school's students are bused, not an uncommon statistic among network schools (only Oak Park does not bus its high school students). How can proposed additions to the curriculum be accommodated within this reality?

Three schools—Page, San Rafael, and Pinellas Park—have discussed going from a seven- to a six-period day. Both California and Florida have discussed going to a seven-period day, but lack of money (again) has deferred this change. Page would like a seven-period day but not unless a 55-minute class period can be maintained. But how can this be done, given the busing schedule? A lengthened school day may be the answer, but the question then becomes, "Will the Arizona legislature mandate such a change?" Thus, the constraining factors become more and more intertwined.

Four schools cited individual and group resistance to change. The problems of turf and territoriality were mentioned as the natural resistance to any change that would have the potential of reducing any department's share of the enrollment. Another school suggested that tradition is both a plus and a minus. Tradition offers continuity and pride; however, "you have to start slow in a school with this much tradition and gradually make inroads." In all schools it's "hard to break the comfortable habits."

For a few schools, being part of a larger district can be a constraint. "When you have a citywide curriculum that applies to every school, it's hard to bring about change." The Woodlawn Dimensions group, as a part of the Baltimore County School System, reported that it is limited as to the type of changes that it could effect on county curriculum:

> Curriculum changes can certainly be suggested, but only the Department of Curriculum, under the auspices of the board, can rightfully implement change in our school; therefore, while the group did not develop new curricula as such, they did constructively take advantage of the county's guidelines . . .

Declining enrollments (usually married to finances or the need to restructure) were also mentioned as a problem for several districts. As one example, San Rafael has gone from a high school population of 4,500 in 1973 to approximately 2,500 today, with a predicted 1,200 students in 1992. This means school consolidations and changes in grade placement and teacher assignments such as took place in Ventura when 9th grade students were moved to the two high schools. It also means RIFs.

For the most part, recently published critiques of the American high school did not seem to constrain the project schools. Several of the reports were familiar to project teachers, who had heard about them at the network meetings. The College Board's *Academic Preparation for College,* for example, had found its way into the deliberations of some of the schools as they developed models and common learnings. Others, such as Ted Sizer's *Horace's Compromise: The Dilemma of the American High School,* had not yet been published.

By far the most discussed work was *A Nation at Risk.* People were divided about its impact. As mentioned earlier, some people were thankful that it had brought many of education's problems to the public's attention. Others, particularly in schools with significant numbers of students who do *not* go on to college, saw it as the "College-Bound Elite at Risk."

> It hurts us because it emphasizes the curriculum for the college bound, not a strong program of general education for all students.

The Importance of the Network

Somewhere in our interviews with people in the project schools, we asked if participation in the project had been worthwhile. In their final reports, the schools had been asked to give their "overall esti-mate of [their] participation in the project" by responding to a five-point scale. Ten schools responded, with six ranking this item a "4" and four giving it a "5," the highest scores given any item on the scale. Even so, we wondered, had all this network activity really made a difference? And if ASCD were to do it again, or if any other organiza-tion were to establish a similar network, what improvements could they make?

The first responses were usually remarks such as:

It was an honor to be selected as a member of the study.

We were proud to be part of a special project.

It was a hell of an investment for our town.

"Why?" we asked.

It gave us new ideas and contacts. We got to talk to people with similar problems. We felt good about the positive things that we did here in our own district.

It was stimulating [to attend the network meetings]. It fired us up, and we wanted to do something after we heard the speakers. It gave us a chance to compare notes.

It was excellent to be part of the network for the rethinking that we have all done.

We wouldn't have gotten as far as we did [in the process] without the network. The nice thing was that we could see our own problems in other schools. The network's outstanding speakers gave us new strength and vigor.

The ASCD network made our people aware of broader horizons, and it helped us to raise our students' expectations.

It renewed me (remarked one administrator).

The project showed us how to play a role in the process of rebuilding/restoring public confidence in education.

Local school districts need help, and ASCD gave us a lot of expertise.

The whole project helped us to move from high schools that are change-resistant to high schools that are change-persistent.

Two districts now felt that they would like to share nationally what they had done locally—their findings, models, processes, and suc-cesses. A steering committee member remarked,

We've already spoken to all the county superintendents, and we got a good response!

And now a word from the other side:

Being part of the network didn't make that much of a difference, but we probably would have withered without it.

The meetings with the other principals were interesting, but I didn't get that much from the network. We didn't get the major themes from the meetings. We never did get to how the school can help teachers to do better.

We need to come back together in a year or two to see if these network schools really do continue what they say they are doing.

We were disappointed that ASCD didn't give us more guidance, but maybe that was unrealistic.

We knew that most of the schools at Wingspread had their own agendas, but we weren't sure what ASCD wanted.

Both those schools that were very positive about the network and those that had reservations agreed that the process had room for improvement. They wanted more communication with the other schools, and principals wanted the chance to share with colleagues who had similar problems.

There really wasn't enough network interaction.

We needed more participatory meetings and less being talked at.

Tell any new network to get as many people involved in their schools as soon as possible.

Any new network needs better articulation about what the schools are doing. Use a WATTS line, regional meetings, and interactive video so people can get together and talk about the grit issues. Money should be made available so that schools can exchange teams of five to six people who can share their innovative ideas. Too much of the burden for arranging things was put on the schools by ASCD. Stress that there has to be *more sharing!*

How can we reap the benefits from what other schools and teachers have done? We should share our common learnings since others may come up with things we haven't thought about. There should be some common learnings that are common to all schools.

Several schools wondered what was going to happen after this report was published. What kind of follow-up evaluation would be done? Several people told us that evaluation is the real "sleeper" when it comes to change both at the project school level and at the network level. The project schools are not yet ready for it, but when it is done it will give schools the data to effect further change. "Data is a powerful tool," one superintendent proclaimed, "and I want people to own their own data and to look at what they can do with it."

Three schools wanted annual reunions, as one put it, "to report on progress and changes from this effort." In another school someone suggested that a new process is needed in order to measure the scope of implementation. "In two years we should get together and reexamine our common learnings." As Pinellas County Assistant Superintendent of Secondary Education Kenneth Webster so aptly put it:

> If we do our homework now and continue to reexamine what goes into general education, we won't have to have another *A Nation at Risk* report in ten years.

6 Conclusions and Recommendations

Modern education is competitive, nationalistic, and separative. It has trained the child to regard material values as of major importance, to believe that his nation is also of major importance and superior to other nations and peoples. The general level of world information is high but usually biased, influenced by national prejudices, serving to make us citizens of our nation but not of the world.   —Albert Einstein

The ASCD general education network project, conducted 1981-1983, antedated the wave of national reports that appeared toward the end of the project. ASCD deliberately chose networking as a leadership strategy because we believed we could make a greater contribution to improving the American high school by actually engaging a group of interested schools in the process of totally redesigning the curriculum. These high schools carried out their work over the two years with real people: faculties, students, parents, and local boards of education. Recognizing the complexity and individuality of local schools, we thought networking provided a significant test of the time-honored notion that local schools should have command of their destinies in curriculum development.

The results documented in this book suggest that local faculties will take seriously their responsibility to the students they serve. We think time will show that the results of such ownership in a school improvement process will be much more enduring than mandated change from above. This is not to say that the state departments do not have a significant role and responsibility for ensuring quality education, nor does it suggest that the federal government should not offer strong leadership on educational issues of national significance. However, we do contend that the task of giving full definition to those common learnings appropriate to all youth in a particular community can best be performed at the local level if teachers are to fully understand and commit to such a common core of learnings.

The network schools could not help but be influenced significantly by the extensive legislation under consideration throughout the states during the period of the project. The schools had to contend with major increases in science and mathematics requirements for graduation even when such mandates were contrary to local faculty or board of education judgment. After the laws were passed, local schools were faced with defining the *kind* of mathematics or science to be taught within a two- or three-year requirement.

As an institution, the high school is amazingly resistant to change, particularly when the impetus comes from outside the school itself. While external observers usually have immediate suggestions as to what *should* be done, rarely do they say *how* the changes are to be made. Rarely does any process emerge that results in substantive improvements. In commenting on the tenacious nature of schools in this respect, Sarason noted: "Particularly in relation to the school culture, our ignorance is vast."[1] Although there were weaknesses in the ASCD networking strategy, we think this strategy can and will be perfected in the future. We feel that the diversity in results that emerged from the network schools demonstrates the efficacy of the process.

One outcome common to the reports of both Ernest Boyer and Ted Sizer is the attempt to provide modest financial assistance to certain high schools that agree to attempt implementation of some of the significant ideas contained in their reports. Foundations have usually approached institutional change and innovation in this way; however, to the extent that this approach is viewed by local faculties as the *imposition* of change, long-term results will probably be minimal. At least this seems to be a lesson from John Goodlad's experience with the League of Schools in Southern California a few years ago.

"The messages of research on curriculum implementation are unequivocal: very little implementation will take place even in positive environments by highly motivated people *unless* training is provided . . ."[2] This summary position by Bruce Joyce reflects a highly significant issue in this project. Many comments made by participants during the network meetings and later in the interviews to Art Roberts suggested high faculty satisfaction with the long hours of curriculum deliberation. But did we create an organizational climate committed to continuous professional growth and improvement? Surely, more impetus to this end occurred in some schools than in others, although our preoccupation with content matters limited the time available for training opportunities in improving teaching itself.

In summary, the project provided a significant effort at school improvement at the high school level that was qualitatively and quantitatively different from the proliferation of reports and mandated changes that occurred during this period. Testimonies of the participants will leave you with a clear impression of the value of engaging in school improvement within a support group such as a network. No school has labeled the project a waste of time. Final judgment must await evidence that a more balanced curriculum is taught and that this curriculum is significantly influencing the lives of students who were part of it.

Conclusions: What the Schools Accomplished

As previous chapters have documented, the network schools went through a somewhat similar series of stages throughout the duration of the project. By the time of the school visits in the fall of 1983, a majority of the schools had made recommendations to their boards of education on graduation requirements and common learnings. Although there was considerable variation in the degree of success, the following discussion represents the major accomplishments of the network schools, even though we cannot attest that *all* schools reached each result. Very often the approaches taken by particular schools included the total secondary curriculum even though our emphasis was limited to general education. That is, attention was often given to a specialized function such as vocational education. Only limited attention was given to school climate, a matter of high concern to students themselves in most schools. However, several of these schools over the years have done significant work in improving school climate.

Adoption of General Education Models

Much attention was given to various conceptions of general education in order to stress a more integrative approach to curriculum. The schools apparently recognized the value in such presentations for developing a starting point in redefining general education. Since many of them experienced enrollment declines and funding shortages during this period, they were or had been involved in reducing course offerings. It was hoped that by developing five or six "clusters" or "broad fields" within their models, more interdisciplinary teaching would be encouraged. While there was some evidence that this did happen, the more important value to the schools was to ensure comprehensiveness and balance in the general education curriculum they were to develop.

More Academic Courses Required

Clearly, the release of *A Nation at Risk* gave national impetus to a movement already under way to require a more academic kind of education of all youth. Although the ASCD network formally disbanded shortly after release of the Secretary of Education's commission report in April 1983, the member schools had already come up with similar recommendations. Many of the schools recommended raising the total units required for graduation, apparently recognizing merit in the criticism that the high school curriculum had not been sufficiently challenging.

In addition, more science and mathematics courses were to be required in most schools, as well as more requirements in social studies and English. The chief impact of such changes in course requirements was likely to be on students of lesser academic aptitude. Thus, while many schools raised the number of units to be required for graduation from 18 to 20 or 22, a recent study reported by the National Center for Education Statistics in the 1984 *Condition of Education*[3] showed that the average senior in 1982 completed 22.4 units of credit at graduation. Even in this period well before the current reform era, the "average" student also had earned more than three years of science and social studies and more than two and one-half years of mathematics.

An Extensive Number of Processes to Involve People Were Used

Early discussions during network meetings revealed what at times seemed an excessive preoccupation with the development of processes necessary to involve faculty, students, the board, and community members. As the project went along, it became apparent how truly necessary this time-consuming process was in generating commitment to the final outcomes. The network members took this responsibility seriously, spending many hours of discussion with the stakeholders in the curriculum. Teachers both enjoyed and profited from the opportunity to discuss and share their thoughts about the real issues of education and thought that these moments should be nurtured and encouraged in the future. Improved communication and sharing were important. Although undue compromises in designing the curriculum may result, perhaps the larger view is that these compromises simply reflect the diversity of viewpoints about the proper role of schools and/or the political nature of curriculum development. In many cases, this process gave the various departments of a high school a more accurate perspective, if nothing else, on what the real curriculum is in the school and, as a result, helped to build a stronger sense of community in several of the schools. The process also helped to develop new leaders who were instrumental in the success of several of the programs.

Common Learnings Were Developed for All Students

For most schools the project provided the first opportunity to give concerted attention to developing the expectations or common learnings held for all students in each major field. By striving to reach consensus on the most important content issues, participants felt they had accomplished much more than simply debating how many units of this course or that were needed. A variety of procedures were used to judge what knowledge is of most worth, and the study groups did examine changing college entrance requirements, the demands of testing, and societal and personal needs. This phase of the project consumed an enormous amount of time and represents the major task that remains when additional requirements in various subjects are mandated from the top down. We agree with Ted Sizer and others that "more is less" and that we ought to be teaching fewer concepts in more depth rather than covering too much material that is rapidly forgotten.

These modest accomplishments represent faculty and community consensus on the most promising steps for them, which are both feasible and in the best interests of their students. In a complex institution such as a high school with a wide variety of professional concerns at stake, change does come in modest increments unless a more persuasive case is made for needed changes than was done in this project. Nevertheless, significant improvement in balance and comprehensiveness of the secondary curriculum *did* result from local community efforts.

What the Project Did Not Accomplish

In looking back on the efforts ASCD made in contributing to network activities, we can easily see how we might have done more, both to address the goals of the project and to respond to logical outgrowths of project goals. Time was, of course, a major restraint; and taking on too much increases the danger of diluting the original goals.

Only limited attention was given to the *improvement of teaching* itself. Participants periodically expressed concern over this issue, saying that if they didn't do a better job in using appropriate teaching strategies for their new program of general education, it would not have as much impact on students as they would like. Although a number of the schools did have a variety of staff development activities under way, these were not necessarily a result of the ASCD project, since our primary attention was on curriculum development.

Although some effort was made to provide a *futures perspective to curriculum planning*, it is difficult to assert that this had much direct effect. Participants agreed on the importance of "learning how to learn" and on developing improved "thinking skills." Major contributions were made by Robert Bundy in examining future life styles and by Herman Kahn on helping students analyze complex global problems, but the curriculum consequences of such issues were not always immediately clear. What did become clear was the unanimity on the necessity of providing students with fundamental learning tools: written composition, critical reading and thinking abilities, and mathematical competencies. The network schools were already involved in computer education with various degrees of commitment, but a few spelled out their expectations more thoroughly as a result of this project.

During the project, *university involvement* was less than we would have liked to have seen. Lack of proximity to a university was often a factor. University professors who have scholarly interest in their fields can give the schools a perspective that is much needed. Increasingly, many communities are availing themselves of this valuable resource.

While the network concern for adopting a general education model clearly implied more *interdisciplinary teaching,* this remains a difficult area to penetrate. A few schools made a start here, but overall we do not find this to be a major accomplishment. Progress may yet occur as the schools continue their work. Nevertheless, it remains an important consideration as the nature of knowledge and our understanding of most topics is recognized to be interdisciplinary.

We definitely learned that *continuity of activity and communication* needs to be sustained among members of a network if it is to attain maximum effectiveness. The members need to have an active role in guiding network affairs. A regular line of communication through a computer linkage, a telephone hot line, or a conventional newsletter can help to inform members and help maintain momentum throughout the life of the project. We were limited by a lack of staff time to make periodic visits to the schools, but communication would be enhanced by more exchanges or visits among the network members themselves. Future ASCD network activity will no doubt profit from the lessons learned through the general education project.

In setting up the network, we hoped to see the member schools create more balanced and comprehensive programs. To this end, we introduced the participants to speakers such as Ernest Boyer, Harry Broudy, and Mortimer Adler. However, we must wonder if in doing so, did we stack the deck? We saw *little movement toward real diversity* in redefining general education, nothing that was very radical. Did we push people too much in one direction, a direction that at the moment is very popular? Certainly, the project reports do not show the diversity to be found in the now classic *Eight Year Study* (1933-1941),[4] when schools tried to improve their curricula, to make them more alive and pertinent by trying a host of different approaches, which today we generally accept as having encouraged student growth. Did we allow enough room for individual differences, learning styles, and the kinds of options that Mary Raywid[5] has discussed in her work?

Recommendations

This report describes a major effort by ASCD to redefine general education for all youth served in 17 high schools from various communities across the land. The common charge in the 80s has been that schools have gone soft, that students are not challenged sufficiently. Antidotes being mandated tend to be mass solutions; for example, requiring *all* students to take three years of science. And that science is usually a college preparatory course, even though forecasts indicate that the demand for engineers is already expected to exceed supply.

Further, *A Nation at Risk* blames the schools for a decline in productivity. To offset the decline, governors and legislators have taken action to require more science and mathematics of all students presumably so that more "high-tech" workers will be available in their states. But the persuasive evidence is that a relatively small number of such jobs will develop in the next decade. This cannot be good policy based on the information at hand today.

Today's youth is the first generation of students for whom the prospects of attaining even the same social class or material wealth as their parents is grim—and many know it. Communities have faced an alarming rate of suicides as well as a rise in alcoholism and drug abuse. The pressures students face seem to be enormous. The family is not the secure institution it once was. The future is crowded with threats of nuclear destruction and environmental catastrophe.

Although they desperately need role models in their lives, today's adolescents spend remarkably little time with adults. A recently reported study of Illinois teenagers showed that they spend less than two percent of their total day with adults other than their parents, about two hours per week with their mothers and a half hour per week with their fathers.[6] Their time is spent with television, socializing, and school, an institution that they often dislike. Adults despair that today's youth want "something for nothing" and are unwilling to delay gratification by sacrificing for an important endeavor or goal.

ASCD sponsored this project out of a belief that the secondary curriculum was in danger of becoming trivialized as a result of preoccupation with minimal competencies. ASCD was also concerned that the curriculum had become overstuffed and badly fragmented by the diverse demands that were being made upon it. In looking at these issues, we believe the project was successful—the thousands of hours of deliberation were not trivial and the nobler purposes of the high school were surely pursued in developing a balanced and comprehensive program of general education for all youth. Given the uncertainty of the possible futures projected for the world of work and leisure, we believe schools must demonstrate their concern for the education of our future citizens by serious consideration of the following recommendations, which grew out of our experiences with the network schools.

Recommendation One: Seek Consensus on the High School's Mission

Recent studies on the American high school have yielded different perceptions of what the central mission of the high school should be and what is really worth knowing. For Mortimer Adler it would be a focus on the classics for all youth, for Ted Sizer it would be intellectual development, while for Freeman Butts it would be civic education. Critics have long lamented the fact that high schools have tried to do far more than they could reasonably expect to accomplish and as a result have diluted the academic program. Recent studies of the ethos or culture of successful companies in the private sector reveal that their mission is clear and known by all employees. We believe there is a lesson for schools in this: if we involve all the stakeholders in the curriculum and if we involve skillful educational leadership in the process, we can develop mission statements for schools that give clear direction to curriculum design and instructional focus. In short, this is what we think is important, this is what we are going to do, and now we will decide how to do it.

Recommendation Two: Set Policy Ensuring Periodic Redesign of the Curriculum

A number of districts already have policies requiring a curriculum review cycle that periodically requires a careful evaluation of instruction in the major fields, followed by appropriate revisions of the curriculum. Our experience with this project suggests that these data may be compared with the recommendations of scholars in the various fields, shifts in life styles, employment opportunities, and social or personal needs. New tools such as strategic planning can help schools engage in what is called "environmental scanning" or "trend analysis" to help educators recognize or anticipate changes affecting what the schools should be teaching.

Recommendation Three: Set Curriculum Balance as a Top Priority in Curriculum Development

Schools have always been victims of whimsy, trends, and political intrusions. These influences on precious instructional time can quickly lead toward imbalance in the curriculum and can thus deprive students of a comprehensive program of general education. For example, the current reform movement does not afford the humanities a very high priority, yet our experience with the network revealed that community members and faculty members believe the arts should be required of *all* students. Less attention is also being afforded health and physical education, even though these are fields usually required by state law and are needed if we still believe in the ancient educational ideal, *mens sana in corpore sano*. As current proposals call for two thirds or three fourths of the time to be spent on the core curriculum, there is now less time left for electives. Good policy development on general education will ensure that students do have time to pursue particular interests in greater depth during their high school years.

Recommendation Four: Develop an Ongoing Program of Staff Development

The number of high school aged young people will continue to decrease nationally for at least another decade. In many sections of the country this means more school closings, fewer new teachers who will be hired, and more teachers with limited seniority who will be RIFed. The end result will be aging faculties who will need to be re-trained to meet curricula and instructional changes such as those outlined in this book. The occasional random workshop can be anticipated to have little effect on anyone. Systematic, well-thought-out programs that reflect systemwide and teacher-identified needs must be organized and made continuously available. It is imperative that teachers play a major role in the development of these programs, because without their interest, enthusiasm, and involvement very little development will take place. This study has highlighted some common learnings that have already led to programs of staff development — interdisciplinary teaching, schoolwide oral communication, and others. In addition, we suggest that there are two immediate areas of major national concern.

1. *Develop Instructional Training Opportunities to Help Teachers Be More Successful with Unmotivated Youth and Potential Dropouts.* A probable consequence of requiring more students to enroll in academic subjects will be increased numbers of youths who are unable to become interested in their classes. For reasons that are not

entirely clear, we have already witnessed an increase in the national dropout rate — in 1971, 75.7 percent of the 18-year-olds graduated from high school, but in 1982 this number had fallen to 71.7 percent.[7] Very little concern seems to be expressed about this national problem in the efforts being made to restore standards in American education. The dropout rate is much higher in cities and among low-income families and minorities and remains a potentially dangerous national problem. Teachers will need staff development to improve student interest and effort. Such staff development should be an integral part of efforts to redesign the secondary curriculum.

2. *Develop Plans for Teaching to Higher Order Educational Outcomes.* Although this ASCD project focused on common learnings in the various subject fields, we all recognized the legitimacy of the criticism that too much teaching focuses on recall of factual knowledge, much of which is quickly forgotten. Training programs for teachers are becoming available in such areas as critical thinking, problem solving, reasoning, inquiry, and creativity. Additional programs will be forthcoming through ASCD's leadership in this area. If real impact on teaching is to be realized, these programs must focus on the needs of teachers in particular fields, and training efforts must be sustained over a period of years.

Recommendation Five: Develop an Organizational Structure to Ensure Curriculum Development

By realizing that the foundations of curriculum development — the needs of learners, the needs of society, and the nature of knowledge — are constantly changing, a few schools try to "proact" rather than react to these changes. In far too many schools, however, curriculum development is a piecemeal operation that is triggered (with some hyperbole on our part) by the need to respond to the latest demands for reform/change, the need to buy new textbooks, or the imperative of an evaluation team from the central office or the regional accrediting agency. Our children deserve better than this.

The ASCD network schools invested a considerable amount of time and effort in setting up structures and conditions that would encourage the involvement of people in the process of curriculum development. This process engendered feelings of ownership and accomplishment, gains that should not be lost. We strongly suggest that every school develop a *process* that can be used to carry out the policy of periodic redesign of the curriculum. In the simplest terms: get people involved, give them the room to freely discuss what needs to be done, support them in their efforts, and facilitate as much as possible what they come up with.

The development of this process does not necessitate a network. Although there was sharing among the network schools, each school essentially developed its own organizational procedure and patterns for the redefinition process. Since there were commonalities in the stages that the schools passed through, the experiences of the network schools may be helpful. We encourage schools to extrapolate from and build upon their experiences in developing a process to redefine the general curriculum. Although the order may vary, the process should include the following stages:

- Organize a steering committee.
- Define the task and orient the faculty.
- Develop a process for faculty involvement.
- Nurture ownership and leadership.
- Define general education.
- Select/develop a model.
- Elaborate a set of common learnings.
- Evaluate courses/transcripts to see what is being taught.
- Add courses/change graduation requirements.
- Make appropriate changes in course content.
- Elicit board of education action.
- Implement the results.
- Continue to nurture the process.
- Organize an evaluation process.

Two of these stages deserve special attention. Many of the network schools are still working to "make appropriate changes in course content" and to "organize an evaluation process." If each department in a school and each teacher in that department does not examine what is taught in each course, as several of the network schools are now doing, there is a real danger that the agreed-upon common learnings may not have the impact that they should. Like so many school philosophies, they may become well-written statements that are afforded lip service but not followed. Questions need to be asked about courses. What needs to be added, dropped, or changed? How do all the puzzle pieces fit together? How do we evaluate the effectiveness of the changes we have made? These important questions need to be addressed.

Although a network per se is not a necessity in rethinking the curriculum, it may be helpful. High schools may want to consider setting up their own informal networks. Schools may share with neighboring school systems. Regional service agencies, if available, can help in setting up a network. State universities are yet another resource to tap, as are state departments of education.

Recommendation Six: Provide Sufficient Time to Design Common Learnings for All Students

Our experience suggests that two to three years is the minimum needed to thoroughly examine all the major fields in general education and to provide opportunities for community participation in the process. The current pattern of mandating so many years of this or that subject should be halted and time provided first to develop the key curriculum concepts to be taught and then to select the teaching strategies to be used.

Once this work has been completed, additional time will be needed to make changes in course content, organize staff development, decide on evaluation procedures, and so on. If the experience of the ASCD network schools is representative, the entire process will take three to five years.

We believe attention to these six elements is crucial if genuine, substantive improvements are to accrue to efforts to redesign general education in the American high school. Our responsibility to future generations is enormous, and our mission ought to be to make sure that the high school is a central and significant institution in the life of the adolescent. We must take seriously our responsibility to do all that is possible to help develop thinking, caring citizens who will be able to lead productive lives in the future as they take their places in the world.

APPENDIX Pinellas Park High School's

Common Learnings

1. An understanding of American cultural roots.
2. Comparison of American institutions with those of other countries (churches, families, schools, and so on).
3. Comparison of cultural expressions such as art, music, architecture.
4. Comparison of economic, social, and political systems of the world.
5. Development of the concept of a global society (instant communication, rapid transportation, and so on).
6. An understanding of the effects of ethnic plurality within our culture.
7. Development of criteria for evaluating art forms.
8. Experience in evaluating art forms.
9. Awareness of the relationship of the arts to a society.
10. Experience with both functional and aesthetic art forms.
11. An understanding of the role that the mass media play in delivering art forms.
12. Experiences that foster creativity.
13. An understanding of the geographical environment of various cultures.
14. An awareness of the values of various cultural groups and of how values are modified.
15. An understanding of the impact of events and personalities on the development of various cultures.
16. An understanding of the concepts of individual versus collective good.
17. An understanding of different forms in literature.

18. Experience in cross-cultural themes in literature.
19. Experience with prose, poetry, and drama through reading and listening.
20. Identification of personal priorities through literature.
21. Recognition of literature as a reflection of society.
22. Experiences with literature that lead to understanding of self and others.
23. Use of literature as a basis for writing.
24. An understanding of the basic legal system of the United States (the Constitution).
25. An understanding of the structure and function of national, state, and local governments in the United States.
26. An understanding of the major parties and groups within the United States that exert political power.
27. A recognition of the impact that various organizations and political groups have on world affairs.
28. An understanding of the historical foundations of the United States.
29. An understanding of the impact of chronological events and personalities that have had a major influence on American life.
30. A recognition that scientific experiments and breakthroughs raise serious ethical, political, and religious questions that demand resolution.
31. A recognition that responsible planning is necessary if technology is to reflect humanitarian values.
32. An understanding of processes by which changes in society take place.
33. An understanding of one's own geographical location in relation to the rest of the world.
34. An understanding of the ways in which geography affects life styles, costs of goods and services, and values.
35. An understanding that citizenship demands responsible behavior.
36. An understanding of the individual rights and responsibilities granted by the Bill of Rights.
37. An understanding that the right to vote is both a privilege and a responsibility.

38. An understanding that a democratic society can function only when laws are respected.
39. An understanding of American governmental revenue sources and uses.
40. An understanding of the effect of resources on world economics.
41. An understanding of the effect of monetary fluctuations on world economics.
42. An understanding that there is a direct relationship between a society's standard of living and its productivity.
43. An understanding of the "Puritan Work Ethic."
44. An awareness of the value of career exploration and planning.
45. An understanding of the importance of the family in the structure of society.
46. A development of skills for parenting and family living.
47. An understanding of the importance of involvement in community life.
48. Development of an attitude of tolerance toward peoples and ideas that are different.
49. An understanding of the concept of limited natural resources.
50. An understanding of the need to develop alternate resources.
51. An understanding of the worldwide effect of conservation and distribution of resources.
52. An understanding of the relationship between resources and population.
53. An understanding of the need to develop a social conscience toward the sharing of resources.
54. An understanding of the physical characteristics of the universe.
55. An understanding of the effect of pollutants.
56. An understanding of the importance of nutrition, exercise, and other health habits.
57. An awareness of individual differences in growth and development.
58. The development of a positive self-concept.
59. An understanding of the relationship between mental and physical health.
60. An awareness of rational thinking as it influences behavior.
61. An understanding of stress and its control.

62. An understanding of basic anatomy and physiology.
63. A knowledge of the effects of drugs and other harmful substances.
64. An understanding of the importance of responsible sexual behavior.
65. Development of skills for maintaining lifelong physical fitness.
66. A recognition that recreation (using talents, aptitudes, interests, and so on) promotes both physical and mental health.
67. Development of skills in safety.
68. Development of skills in first aid.
69. Understanding of basic computer operations (input, retrieval, reading printouts, and so on).
70. An understanding that the computer is controlled by the programmer.
71. The responsible use of computer information.
72. Identification of various electronic communications systems.
73. An understanding of the impact of instant and dynamic media on opinion and decision making.
74. An understanding of subliminal media influences.
75. An understanding of the relationship between electronic communications and individual privacy.
76. An understanding of ways in which electronic communications affect individuals.
77. An understanding of the effects of time management on productivity, efficiency, and health.
78. An understanding of ways to develop time management plans.
79. An understanding of the processes of problem solving.
80. Opportunities to practice problem solving and to experience the outcome.
81. An understanding of and experience in logical thinking.
82. The ability to collect and analyze data.
83. Competence in identifying criteria for academic success.
84. An understanding of the value of constructive criticism.
85. Experiences that foster the pursuit of excellence.
86. Competence in identifying themes and main ideas.
87. Competence in note-taking.
88. Competence in organizing study materials and outlining.

89. An understanding of the importance of controlling the study environment.
90. Competence in use of addition, subtraction, multiplication, and division in problem solving involving whole numbers, fractions, and decimals.
91. Competence in use of traditional and metric measurement systems.
92. Competence in word recognition.
93. Competence in reading with comprehension.
94. Competence in reading at an appropriate rate.
95. Competence in analyzing reading materials.
96. A recognition that there are different purposes for writing.
97. The ability to use Standard English in writing.
98. The ability to express ideas in both a formal and an informal style.
99. Competence in usage and skills of editing.
100. Recognition of conversation as an important element of oral communication.
101. Recognition that communication involves both listening and speaking.
102. Competence in presentation of ideas orally.
103. An understanding of the different purposes for viewing.
104. An understanding of the elements and importance of critical viewing.
105. Development of practical living skills.

APPENDIX Ames High School's

B Elements of General Education*

Values and Beliefs

1. Knowledge of the premises inherent in personal and social values and beliefs, of how to make responsible decisions, and of the importance of participating in discussions of ethical and moral issues.
2. Knowledge of how laws, customs, traditions (agreed-upon behaviors) contribute to personal and social continuity.
3. Knowledge of the distinction between beliefs and facts.
4. Knowledge of how personal and social values and beliefs are formed, passed on, and revised.
5. Knowledge that the values and beliefs that guide individuals and society are a result of human choices and tradition.
6. Knowledge of how political ideologies and religion have shaped the values and beliefs of the individual and society.
7. Knowledge of what social values are currently held and socially enforced, and how society reacts to controversial beliefs. This includes the concern for multicultural, non-sexist education.
8. Knowledge of the need for continuous investigation and evaluation of values and beliefs, both personal and social.

Time and Tradition

1. Knowledge of our common heritage.
2. Knowledge of essential ideas and events that have shaped the course of history.

*Adapted from: Ernest L. Boyer and Arthur Levine, *A Quest for Common Learning* (Washington, D.C.: Carnegie Foundation, 1981), pp. 35-44.

3. Knowledge of the convergence and divergence of social, political, economic, scientific, and religious forces.
4. Inquiry into the nature of freedom, authority, conformity, rebellion, war, peace, rights, responsibilities, equality, and exploitation.
5. Inquiry into the interrelationships among ideas and cultures.
6. Knowledge of the processes that cause societal change.
7. Learning how to cope with change and anticipate the future.

Groups, Institutions, and Cultures

1. Recognizing that a community is a collection of institutions and groups, such as educational, economic, familial, political, religious.
2. Recognizing one's own shared groups and institutions.
3. Understanding the impact of the origin, evolution, and death of institutions and groups.
4. Understanding interaction of individuals and institutions, including ourselves, and how such interaction both facilitates and complicates our existence.
5. Recognizing the responsibilities of institutional and group membership.
6. Recognizing the responsibilities of individuals toward institutions and groups of which they are members.
7. Recognizing the contribution of different cultures to a common culture.

Producing and Consuming

1. Recognizing individual rights and responsibilities in the management of money, property, and human and natural resources in our economy.
2. Understanding the American system of business and free enterprise and contrasting this with other economic systems.
3. Recognizing that everyone produces and consumes and that, through this process, we as individual, state, or nation are interdependent upon others for a functioning economic system.
4. Developing the ability to make judgments and rational decisions in a variety of life roles.

5. Understanding the roles of work and leisure in our society and their impact on an individual's life style.
6. Exploring vocations and careers compatible with an individual's needs, skills, interests, and abilities.
7. Developing attitudes, skills, and work habits for employment.

Nature and Technology

1. Understanding that every form of life is dependent on other forms of life.
2. Understanding the development and structure of the human being.
3. Understanding the basic structures and the natural laws of our physical world.
4. Understanding the limitations of the physical world and the finite nature of resources.
5. Understanding how science is a process of trial and error; how, through observation and testing, theories are found, refined, sometimes discarded, and often give rise to other theories.
6. Understanding the pervasive influence of science and technology on all our lives, including the effect of mass communication.
7. Understanding that the development of science and technology has led to both benefit and risk to humankind.
8. Recognizing the areas where humans can control nature and where nature is immune to human control.
9. Recognizing the interrelationships of ethics, morality, and technology.

Aesthetics

1. Understanding how we communicate in such areas as music, dance, and visual arts.
2. Understanding how we communicate through verbal and non-verbal signs/signals.
3. Understanding the function of symbols within cultures.

APPENDIX Oak Park and River Forest High School's

C Listing of General Education Experiences

The learning experiences in common for all students should develop *skills for lifelong learning* by:

1. Providing competence in symbolical language, including written, oral, visual, and mathematical.
2. Teaching how to locate, assimilate, synthesize, and process information.
3. Teaching how to conceptualize and utilize ideas.
4. Developing an understanding of methods and problem solving.
5. Preparing for understanding, influencing, and adjusting to change.
6. Providing alternate and varied ways to learn.
7. Encouraging the ability to create images, forms, and ideas.

The learning experiences in common for all students should foster a sense of *global consciousness* by:

8. Providing an understanding and appreciation of the heritage of our country, including the literary, artistic, political, economic, and historical. ("Philosophical" and "scientific" were added later.)
9. Providing an understanding and appreciation of the contributions made to world civilization by non-Western and other Western cultures, including the literary, artistic, political, economic, and historical. ("Philosophical" and "scientific" were added later.)
10. Producing an awareness of the interdependencies that exist among individuals and nations.
11. Showing how the past has affected the present, and how the past and the present help determine the future.

12. Developing a sense of responsibility as citizens of the world, the nation, and the community.
13. Developing an appreciation of universal values such as honesty, justice, and kindness. (This item was eventually dropped.)

The learning experiences in common for all students should engender a *sense of self-worth* by:

14. Encouraging the establishing of personal goals, the making of decisions leading toward those goals, and the accepting of consequences of those decisions.
15. Enabling the building upon personal strength and the recognizing of personal weaknesses.
16. Encouraging growth in relationships with others, both competitively and cooperatively.
17. Encouraging the recognition and acquisition of good health in all of its aspects.
18. Creating experiences that will enable students to know and value success.
19. Encouraging aspirations to do the very best.
20. Developing attitudes and habits needed in the world of work and play.

APPENDIX Ventura High School's

D Requirements for Success

"What I am going to be is up to me."

Success Requirements at Ventura High School

1. Attend class and be on time.
2. Be prepared.
3. Complete assignments.
4. Respect yourself and others.

Student Responsibilities

Students at Ventura High School are considered to be fully responsible for themselves, and they know that everything they do, or they don't do, is *by choice*. They will take credit for success as well as failure, regardless of how people treat them.

Staff Responsibilities

We acknowledge that we have the obligation of providing materials and assignments that are relevant, realistic, and appropriate for the students.

Evaluation of Performance

Each quarter grade will include evaluation of your demonstrated *abilities* in (1) success requirements, (2) speaking and listening skills,

(3) writing, (4) spelling, (5) math, (6) reading, (7) understanding of the particular subject area.

Promise of the School

To help each student in fulfilling the requirements for a diploma from VHS by being supportive, encouraging, and friendly.

Statement of Success

SUBJECT: Geometry _____ TEACHER: _____

BASIC OBJECTIVES OF THE COURSE. To develop in each student:
1. Habits in logical and precise reasoning to form conclusions based on established facts.
2. Usable, practical applications of the scientific laws found in geometry.
3. Understanding of the fundamental properties of points, lines, and plane figures.
4. Logical and precise thinking in the field of mathematics, which should eventually apply to life in general.

ASSIGNMENTS TO BE SUCCESSFULLY COMPLETED IN ORDER TO RECEIVE CREDIT FOR THE COURSE (Class and Homework Policy):

Daily assignments are an integral part of the course. The normal procedure will be to review the previous day's work prior to carefully introducing any new material. Time will usually be available to begin the new assignment in class, but approximately 30 minutes of outside homework will be required to be successful. Assignments will be turned in for credit.

DISCIPLINE PROCEDURES—WHAT WILL HAPPEN IF YOU CHOOSE NOT TO FOLLOW THE SUCCESS REQUIREMENTS:

Conscientious class attendance is expected as daily classroom discussions and explanations are essential to successful completion of this course. VHS attendance, truancy, and tardy policies will be closely followed.

GRADING POLICY:
   Grading will consist of the following areas:
1. Homework assignments (approximately 20-25% of point total).
2. Tests (approximately 75-80% of point total).
3. Classroom attendance and participation (subjective evaluation).
4. Optional extra credit projects and problems.

Statement of Success

SUBJECT: U.S. History _____   TEACHER: _____

BASIC OBJECTIVES OF THE COURSE:
   Students will have the opportunity to:
1. Appreciate their American heritage and the rights and privileges guaranteed by the U.S. Constitution.
2. Appreciate the importance of understanding the past as a prerequisite for coping with the present and anticipating the future.
3. Appreciate the multi-cultural and multi-ethnic forces (with special emphasis on British republicanism and common law) that have shaped the American society.
4. Understand the relationship between freedom and responsibility.
5. Be exposed to the processes by which societies develop and change.
6. Examine the directional forces that determine the process of a free or mixed economic system.

ASSIGNMENTS TO BE SUCCESSFULLY COMPLETED IN ORDER TO RECEIVE CREDIT FOR THE COURSE (Class and Homework Policy):
1. Each student will keep a functional notebook.
2. Each student will prepare written reports on topics of historical value. These reports will be assigned on a quarterly basis.
3. Written homework will be assigned only as needed; however, reading assignments from the textbook or other materials will be given on a daily basis.
4. Quizzes, chapter tests, and quarterly examinations will be given as appropriate.

DISCIPLINE PROCEDURES—WHAT WILL HAPPEN IF YOU CHOOSE NOT TO FOLLOW THE SUCCESS REQUIREMENTS:

In terms of tardies, truancies, and so on, we will follow the procedures developed by Ventura High School. Generally, disruptive behavior will not be tolerated in the classroom. Students who cannot or will not conform to the rules noted above will be asked to report to the Guidance Center for corrective action or reassignment to another U.S. History class.

GRADING POLICY:

Complete the basic assignments suggested above. All assignments will be awarded a point total, and the academic grade will be developed by evaluation of the total points earned by a student (90%, 80%, 70%, 50% are the bottom level percentages for grades A through D).

80% of the total student grade will be based upon the student's academic grade; the other 20% of the grade will be based upon teacher evaluation of such items as general behavior, class participation, and so on.

Statement of Success

SUBJECT: English 106 _____   TEACHER: _____

BASIC OBJECTIVES OF THE COURSE:
1. To write complex sentences over 12 words in length; to write seven-sentence paragraphs using topic sentence and adequate support; to write a five-paragraph essay.
2. To spell the 1,000 most misspelled words and other advanced terms found in literature.
3. To learn grade level vocabulary words, 100 prescribed plus those gleaned through literature.
4. To read culturally enriching poetry, short stories, plays, essays, novels, and biographies.
5. To avoid common mistakes in punctuation, capitalization, number agreement, verb tenses.

ASSIGNMENTS TO BE SUCCESSFULLY COMPLETED IN ORDER TO RECEIVE CREDIT FOR THE COURSE (Class and Homework Policy):
1. Submit over 60% of the assignments with a passing grade of 60% or more.
2. Participate orally in class discussions.
3. Conform to school policies.

DISCIPLINE PROCEDURES—WHAT WILL HAPPEN IF YOU CHOOSE NOT TO FOLLOW THE SUCCESS REQUIREMENTS:
1. After formal warning, further offenses will require a 15-minute detention for each offense that day.
2. Parent/guardian contact through phone or letter.
3. Redirection of misconduct through counselor mediation.

GRADING POLICY:
90%+ = A
80% = B
70% = C
60% = D
Plus deviate citizenship could cost one full grade.

Notes

Chapter 1

[1]Gordon Cawelti, *Vitalizing the High School* (Washington, D.C.: Association for Supervision and Curriculum Development, 1974).

[2]Marvin Cetron and Thomas O'Toole. *Encounters With the Future: A Forecast of Life Into the 21st Century* (New York: McGraw-Hill Book Company, 1982).

[3]Government Printing Office, *Monthly Labor Review,* November 1983.

[4]Thomas J. Moore. "Tinker, Tailor, Waitress, Clerk: Is It Worthwhile to Go to College?" *The Washington Post,* October 23, 1983, sec. C, pp. 1-4.

[5]National Commission on Excellence, *A Nation at Risk* (Washington, D.C.: U.S. Department of Education), p. 5.

[6]Gordon Cawelti, "Needed: A Process for Redefining General Education in the American High School," *NASSP Bulletin* 65 (March 1981): 9-15.

[7]ASCD's use of the term "general education" refers to the detailed development of graduation requirements. The same meaning has been given to the term "core curriculum" in several national reports, although historical use of "core" has a somewhat different connotation.

[8]Report of the Harvard Committee, *General Education in a Free Society* (Cambridge, Mass.: Harvard University Press, 1945,), p. 4.

[9]James Conant, *The American High School Today* (New York: McGraw-Hill, 1959), pp. 46-76.

[10]H. S. Broudy, B. O. Smith, and Joe R. Burnett, *Democracy and Excellence in American Secondary Education* (Chicago: Rand McNally, 1964), p. 247.

[11]Ernest L. Boyer and Arthur A. Levine, *A Quest for Common Learning* (Washington, D.C.: Carnegie Foundation for the Advancement of Teaching, 1980).

[12]Gordon Cawelti, "Redefining General Education in the American High School," *Educational Leadership* 39 (May 1982): 570-572.

[13]*Academic Preparation for College — What Students Need To Know and Be Able To Do* (New York: The College Board, 1983).

[14]Ernest L. Boyer, *High School* (New York: Harper and Row, 1983), p. 117.

[15]John I. Goodlad, *A Place Called School* (New York: McGraw Hill Book Company, 1984), p. 187.

[16]Theodore R. Sizer, *Horace's Compromise: The Dilemma of the American High School* (Boston: Houghton Mifflin Company, 1984), p. 132.

Chapter 2

[1]Of the original 17 high schools that began the project, two—Central High School in St. Louis and Will Rogers High School in Tulsa, Oklahoma—were not able to complete the process and a third—Colville High School in Colville, Washington—submitted its report after the interviews had been conducted and too late for inclusion in this report.

[2]"Oak Park and River Forest High School, 1873-1976." (This printed history and a similar example published at East High in Denver are fine examples of civic pride and tradition building.

[3]"109-year-old Oak Park Is a Model of a Comprehensive High School," *Chicago Tribune,* January 8, 1979.

Chapter 3

[1]Charles Dickens, *Tale of Two Cities,* ed. George Woodcock (New York: Penguin Books, Inc., 1970).

[2]Prince Gregory Potemkin, minister, lover, and possibly husband to Catherine the Great, Empress of Russia, was unjustly accused by a foreign ambassador of having set up cardboard villages along the Dneiper River, populated by well-dressed peasants brought there for the occasion so that Catherine, on a boat trip from Kiev to the Crimea, would be impressed by Potemkin's administration of the area.

[3]See the October 1983 issue of ASCD's *Curriculum Update.*

[4]David Weingast, "Shared Leadership—'The Damn Thing Works'," *Educational Leadership* 37 (March 1980): 502-506.

[5]*The Seven Cardinal Principles* (Washington, D.C.: NEA Commission on the Reorganization of Secondary Education, 1918).

[6]Sara Lawrence Lightfoot, *The Good High School* (New York: Basic Books, 1984).

Chapter 5

[1]Paul Berman and others, *Federal Programs Supporting Educational Change, Vol. IV: A Summary of the Findings in Review* (unabridged). USOE, April 1975.

[2]Although Page has not changed its graduation requirements, the state of Arizona has, and this will affect Page. The state has increased the science requirements from one year to two, one year more than Page requires. In adding this requirement, Page will not increase the number of credits required for graduation, but student selection of electives will be restricted by the change.

[3]See the October 1983 issue of ASCD's *Curriculum Update,* p. 4.

[4]In May 1984, just days before this manuscript was completed, the Louisiana legislature mandated new graduation requirements: three years of mathematics, four years of English, three years of science, three and one-half years of social studies, including a year of world history and one-half year in computers.

Chapter 6

[1]Seymour B. Sarason, *The Culture of the School and the Problem of Change* (Boston: Allyn and Bacon, 1982), p. 37.

[2]Bruce Joyce, Richard H. Hersh, and Michael McKibbin, *The Structure of School Improvement* (New York: Longman, 1983), p. 137.

[3]National Center for Education Statistics, *Condition of Education,* 1984 ed. (Washington, D.C.: U.S. Government Printing Office, 1984), p. 59.

[4]Wilford M. Aikin, *The Story of the Eight-Year Study* (New York: McGraw-Hill, 1942).

[5]Mary Anne Raywid, "Synthesis of Research on Schools of Choice," *Educational Leadership* 41 (April 1984): 70-78.

[6]Mihaly Csikzentmihalye and Reed Larson, *Being Adolescent: Conflict and Growth in the Teenage Years* (New York: Basic Books, 1984).

[7]National Center for Education Statistics, *Condition of Education*.